Table of contents

INTRODUCTION

Welcome to the world of Python programming! If you're a complete beginner this is the perfect place for you.

Learning Python opens up a wealth of opportunities in software development, data analysis, web development, artificial intelligence, and much more.

Python is known for its simplicity, readability, and versatility, making it an ideal language for beginners while also being powerful enough to handle complex projects. With its clean and concise syntax, Python allows you to focus on solving problems and writing elegant code without getting bogged down in unnecessary details.

In this guide, we'll take you on a journey through the fundamentals of Python programming, starting from the basics and gradually building up your skills.

You will understanding fundamental programming concepts such as variables, data types, operators, loops, and control structures. Get familiar with the syntax of Python.

We'll take it step by step. We'll make gross errors to be able to correct them and teach you how to avoid them.

Whether you're interested in building web applications, automating tasks, analyzing data, or delving into machine learning, Python has you covered.

So, let's dive in and explore the exciting world of Python programming together. By the end of this guide, you'll have a solid foundation in Python and the confidence to embark on your own coding adventures.

Happy coding!

PYTHON INTERPRETER

Python Interpreter:

What is a python interpreter?

A Python interpreter is a program that translates Python code into machine-readable bytecode and then executes it. It reads Python code line by line, converts it into intermediate code, and then executes the code one instruction at a time. The interpreter is responsible for interpreting the instructions of the Python code and executing them on the computer's hardware.

Python comes with a built-in interpreter that allows you to execute Python code interactively or run Python scripts from the command line. Additionally, there are alternative Python interpreters available, such as IPython, Jupyter Notebook, and PyPy, each offering unique features and capabilities.

What is VS code?

Is "VS code" a python interpreter?

No, Visual Studio Code (VS Code) is not a Python interpreter itself. Instead, VS Code is a source code editor developed by Microsoft, which supports various programming languages including Python. While VS Code provides features such as syntax highlighting, code completion, debugging, and version control integration for Python development, it relies on external Python interpreters to execute Python code.

You can configure VS Code to work with different Python interpreters, such as the standard CPython interpreter, Anaconda, PyPy, or any other interpreter you have installed on your system. Once configured, VS Code can interact with the selected interpreter to execute Python code, debug applications, and provide other development features.

This course will use VS code to edit python code and use interactively the windows terminal to interpret the code.

Functions:

In Python, a function is a block of reusable code that performs a specific task. Functions are used to organize code into manageable and reusable parts, allowing you to break down complex tasks into smaller, more manageable pieces.

A function typically takes some inputs (called parameters or arguments), performs certain operations, and then returns a result. However, not all functions in Python need to return a value.

Basic syntax of a Python function:

```
def function_name(parameters):
    # code block
    # perform operations
    return result
```

• def is a keyword used to define a function.

•;function_name is the name of the function. It should be descriptive of the task the function performs.

For instance, if the function describes how to drink water, its name should be: drink_water instead of d_w.

By convention, a function starts always with a lowercase letter

• parameters (optional) are inputs to the function. They are variables that hold the values passed to the function.

• The code block inside the function is executed when the function is called.

• return statement (optional) specifies the value that the function should return. If omitted, the function returns None

A simple example of a function adding two numbers:

```
def add_numbers(x, y):

    return x + y

result = add_numbers(3, 5)

print(result)

# Output: 8
```

Function is an action that lets you do something in the program. The function uses the program to get the computer do a certain thing.

If you installed "Vs code" and linked the terminal to interpret the code, tape in terminal this: "code hello.py", this will open a new empty file in vs code name "hello.py"

print function:

```
print("hello world")

output : hello world
```

This means that if you enter this script: print("hello world") in your editor , and run it, your interpreter will display: hello world

Output: what's you see after running your code

Argument(s): an input to the function that somehow influence its behavior

Bugs: Mistakes in the program

Input:

```
input("what's your name?")

print("hello world")

output : hello world
```

In this case, what does "**input**" mean? "input" just invites you, the user to interact with your interpreter to do the action between " ". Here it invites you just to enter your name. After entering your name, it will display only this: hello world. That's the action that i, as programmer, asks the program to do.

Variables: stores a value, contains a certain value.

In Python, a variable is a named storage location that holds a value. Variables are used to store data that can be manipulated and accessed within a program. Unlike some other programming languages, Python is dynamically typed, meaning you don't need to explicitly declare the type of a variable before assigning a value to it.

Here's how you can declare and assign values to variables in Python:

```python
x = 5  # Assigns the value 5 to the variable x

name = "Alice"  # Assigns the string "Alice" to the variable name

pi = 3.14  # Assigns the value 3.14 to the variable pi
```

In Python, variable names:

Can contain letters, digits, and underscores (_), but can't start with a digit.

Are case-sensitive (x, X, and "X" are three different variables).

Should be descriptive and meaningful to make the code easier to understand.

You can change the value stored in a variable simply by assigning a new value to it:

```python
x = 5
print(x)  # Output: 5
x = 10  # Change the value stored in x
print(x)  # Output: 10
```

```python
name = input("what's your name")  # here 'name' is a variable
print("hello")
print(name)
```

In this program above, I'm invited to type my name, for instance "Patrick", and it will display this as output:

Hello

Patrick

Comments: Comments are notes in your code that explains what you're doing. This is useful for you and others to provide documentation, explanations and descriptions.

For instance:

Ask user for their name

name = input("what's your name") # here 'name' is a variable

Say hello to user

print("hello")

print(name)

Pseudocode:

Steps of your code. Structure of your code.
Pseudocode is a high-level description of an algorithm or a process written in natural language, resembling the structure of a programming language, but not bound to any specific syntax or conventions. It's used to plan and outline the logic of a solution before actual coding begin.

Example of pseudocode for finding the maximum value in an array:

```
1. Set max_value to the first element of the array
2. For each element in the array:
     If the current element is greater than
max_value:

        Update max_value to the current element

3. Return max_value
```

Function: print()

print function: parameters:

https://docs.python.org/3/library/functions.html#print

Built-in Functions — Python 3.12.2 documentation

code hello.py (this is for creating a new file and opening it).

The command "**code**" in the terminal: is for opening VS code.

Testing our python file in the terminal:

py hello.py or **python hello.py** (depending on how the terminal is configured)

```
1    name = input("what's your name?")
2    print("hello, " + name)
3    print("hello, ",name)
```
py hello.py
what's your name?Patrick

hello, Patrick

Really pay attention when using "py" or "python" you may be using different versions and different environments of python. For example you installed this module: mypy with pip install mypy. But when you run your file "**py hello.py**" you encounter an ModuleError, it's maybe you installed the module in one environment and not in another. In this case you should use "**python hello.py**".

It's useful to know how to use the "print function", because most of your program will use i

```
print(*objects, sep=' ', end='\n',
file=None, flush=False)
```

*objects: can take any number of objects

sep= ' ' : separator

end='\n' : means new line, it creates a new line.

end='\n' is a parameter of the print() function that specifies what character or characters should be printed at the end of each printed line.

By default, the end parameter is set to '\n', which represents a newline character. This means that after printing the content provided to the print() function, python will automatically move to the next line before printing the next content.

For example:

```
1    print("Hello", end='\n')
2    print("World")
```
py hello.py
Hello
World

You can change the value of "**end**" parameter to something else. For example:

```
1    print("Hello", end=' ')
2    print("World")
```
py hello.py

Hello World

Here you can use " " or ' ' (Double quotes, or simple quotes)

sep=' ' : by default, the argument will be separated by single space.

In Python, the sep argument in the print() function specifies the separator between the values that are passed to the function. By default, the sep argument is set to ' ', which means that the values are separated by a space character.

```
1   # Ask user for his name
2   name = input("What's your name?")
3
4   #say hello to user
5   print("hello,", name, sep="")
```
py hello.py
What's your name?Joseph

hello,Joseph

With **end** set on default: print automatically passes on a new line

```
1   # Ask user for his name
2   name = input("What's your name?")
3
4   #say hello to user
5   print("hello,", end="")
6   print(name)
```
py hello.py
what's your name?Joseph

hello,Joseph

```
1   #Say hello to user
2   print("hello,", "friend")
```
py hello.py
hello, friend

Backslash = escape character

```
1    #Say hello to user
2    print("hello,\"friend\"")
```

py hello.py

hello,"friend"

```
1    # Ask user for his name
2    name = input("What's your name?")
3
4    #say hello to user
5    print(f"hello, {name}")
```
py hello.py
What's your name? Joseph

hello, Joseph

f = special string, format in a special way

String Methods:

In Python, a string is a sequence of characters enclosed within either single quotes (') or double quotes ("). Strings are used to represent text data in Python programs.

Example: 'Hello, World!' or "Hello, World!"

https://docs.python.org/3/library/stdtypes.html#string-methods

```
1    #Ask user for his name
2    name = input("what's your name?")
3
4    #Remove white space
5    name = name.strip()
6
7    #Say hello to user
8    print(f"hello,{name}")
```

py hello.py:
what's your name? Eddy

py hello.py:
what's your name?   Eddy

hello,Eddy

For the first output, I did not place any space between Eddy and the question mark, and I did it for the second output, but we still have the same hello,Eddy eventually.

Capitalize() function:

The capitalize() function is a method in Python that is used to capitalize the first letter of a string. It returns a copy of the string with the first character converted to uppercase and all other characters converted to lowercase.

```
1    #Ask user for his name
2    name = input("what's your name?")
3
4    #Capitalize user's name (only the first letter)
5    name = name.capitalize()
6
7    #Remove White space
8    name = name.strip()
9
10   #Say hello to user
11   print(f"hello,{name}")
```

py hello.py:
what's your name?eddy

hello,Eddy

capitalize("hello WORLD") -> Output: Hello world

```
1    #Ask user for his name
2    name = input("what's your name?")
3
4    #Capitalize each first letter of each word
5    name = name.title()
6
7    #Remove White space
8
9    name = name.strip()
10
11   #Say hello to user
12   print(f"hello,{name}")
```

what's your name? eddy london

hello,Eddy London

title() function

The **title()** function is a method in python that is used to capitalize the first letter of each word in a string. It returns a copy of the string with the first letter of each word converted to uppercase and all other characters converted to lowercase.

```python
1    #Ask user for his name
2    name = input("what's your name?")
3
4    #Remove White space from str and capitalize user's name
5    name = name.strip().title()
6
7    #Say hello to user
8    print(f"hello,{name}")
```

py hello.py
what's your name? eddy london
hello,Eddy London

Below, you can make your code even more compact

```python
1    #All in one
2    name = input("what's your name?").strip().title()
3
4    #Say hello to user
5    print(f"hello,{name}")
```

py hello.py
what's your name?eric london
hello,Eric London

```python
1    #Ask user for their name
2    name = input("what's your name?")
3
4    #split user's name into first name and last name
5    first, last = name.split(" ")
6
7    #Say hello to user
8    print(f"hello,{first}")
```

py hello.py

what's your name?eric london
hello,eric

17

INTEGERS (No decimal)

Different operations with integers:

+ , - , * , /

% (this one is modulo, returns the remainder of the division of two numbers)

I can use python as a calculator

x = 1

y = 2

z = x + y

print(z)

Let's go for a new file :

In the terminal: **code calculator.py** →This opens a new python file in VS code

```
1    x = input("what's x ?")
2    y = input("what's y ?")
3
4    z = x+y
5    print(z)
```

py calculator.py

Ouput:
what's x ?5
what's y ?5
55

So, why we do not have 5 + 5 = 10, but instead had 55?

This is because we did not configure our input correctly with **"int"** which means "integer". Here python considered our two numbers as "str" and not "int", so instead, the operation was concatenation.

```
1    x = int(input("what's x ?"))
2    y = int(input("what's y ?"))
3
4    z = x+y
5    print(z)
```

py calculator.py

Ouput:
what's x ?4
what's y ?7
11

This is another way to write the code

```
1    x = int(input("what's x ?"))
2    y = int(input("what's y ?"))
3
4    z = x+y
5    print(z)
```

py calculator.py

Ouput:

what's x ?4

what's y ?7

11

```
1    x = input("what's x ?")
2    y = input("what's y ?")
3
4    z = int(x) + int(y)
5    print(z)
```

FLOAT (decimal)

x = float(input(what's x?))

y = float(input(what's y?))

print(x+y)

docs.python.org/3/library/functions.html#round

round(number[, ndigits]) (ndigits = number of digits)

```
1    x = float(input("what's x?"))
2    y = float(input("what's y?"))
3
4    z = round(x+y)
5    print(f"{z:,}")
```

py calculator.py

what's x?999

what's y?1

1,000

```
1    x = float(input("what's x?"))
2    y = float(input("what's y?"))
3
4    z = round(x/y, 2) # "2" is the number of digits after the comma
5    print(z)
```

py calculator.py

what's x?77

what's y?4

19.25

The equivalence of the code above:

```
1   x = float(input("what's x?"))
2   y = float(input("what's y?"))
3
4   z = x/y
5   print(f"{z:.2f}")
```

This will give the same results

FUNCTION: The keyword "def"

Python gives us the possibility to create our own functions and call them whenever we want.

Let's imagine, we have a function "hello"

"def hello () "

(Let's go back to our file hello.py)

```
1   def hello():
2       print("hello")
3
4   name = input("what's your name?")
5   hello()
6   print(name)
```

py hello.py

what's your name?Stephan

hello

Stephan

The function "hello()" displays only "hello".

Another version with hello (to), we can replace "to" by any name, the result will be the same

```
1    def hello(to):
2        print("hello,",to)
3
4    name = input("what's your name?")
5    hello(name)
```

py hello.py

what's your name?Stephan

hello, Stephan

Version 3

Here, we display first "hello, world"

```
1    def hello(to = "world"):
2        print("hello,",to)
3
4    hello()
5
6    name = input("what's your name?")
7    hello(name)
```

py hello.py

hello, world

what's your name?

hello, Stephan

We can put this function in a "main" function

Here we start we the main() function, then, we enter the name, after we call the function "hello".

22

```
1    def main():
2        name = input("what's your name?")
3        hello(name) # Here we do not have any clue on what the function "hello" really is
4
5    def hello(to = "world"):
6        print("hello, ",to)
7
8    main()
```

py hello.py

what's your name?Stephan

hello, Stephan

In the below code, we will encounter an error, because of the variable "name". A variable defined in the main function can only be used in the main function.

```
1    def main():
2        name = input("What's your name?")
3        hello(name)
4
5    def hello():
6        print("hello,", name)
7
8    main()
```

RETURN

In Python, the return statement is used to exit a function and return a value (or multiple values) back to the caller.

When a function is called, it may perform some computations or operations and produce a result. The return statement allows the function to send that result back to the code that called it.

Example of a function that adds two numbers and returns the result:

```
def add_numbers(x, y):
    return x + y
result = add_numbers(3, 5)
print(result)  # Output: 8
```
In this example:

1. The **add_numbers** function takes two parameters, **x** and **y**.
2. It performs addition of x and y.
3. The return statement is used to send the result of the addition (x + y) back to the caller.

When add_numbers(3, 5) is called, it returns 8, which is then assigned to the variable result.

The return statement can be used to return any data type, including numbers, strings, lists, tuples, dictionaries, or even custom objects.

If a function doesn't explicitly include a return statement, it implicitly returns None.
For example:

```
def say_hello():
    print("Hello")
result = say_hello()
print(result)  # Output: None
```

24

let's try a new file

code power.py → This means if I enter this command on the terminal, it will open a new python file in VS code named **power.py**

```
def main( ) :

        x = int(input ("What's x?"))

        print("X squared is", square(x))

def square(n): #we define the function "square"

        return pow(n,2)

main( )
```

```
py power.py
what's x?9
x squared is 81
```

We have many comparison operators:

> (superior to)

>= (superior or equals to)

< (inferior to)

<= (inferior or equals to)

== (comparison)

!= (not equal)

= (Assignment, compares things from the right to the left)

Conditional "if"

Open a new file : **code compare.py**

```
1    x = int(input("what's x?"))
2    y = int(input("what's y?"))
3
4    if x<y:
5        print("x is less than y")
6    elif x>y:
7        print("x is greater than y")
8    elif x==y:
9        print("x equal to y")
```

py compare.py

what's x?5

what's y?8

x is less than y

We can do the same thing, but this time more concise

```
1    x = int(input("what's x?"))
2    y = int(input("what's y?"))
3
4  ∨ if x<y or x>y:
5          print("x is not equal to y")
6  ∨ else:
7    |    print("x is equal to y")
8
```

py compare.py

what's x?7

what's y?9

x is not equal to y

```
1    x = int(input("what's x?"))
2    y = int(input("what's y?"))
3
4  ∨ if x != y:
5    |    print("x is not equal to y")
6  ∨ else:
7    |    print("x is equal to y")
```

py compare.py

what's x?8

what's y?57

x is not equal to y

Let's create a new file: **code grade.py**

```
1    score = int(input("Score:"))
2
3    if score >= 90 and score <= 100:
4        print("Grade: A")
5    elif score >= 80 and score < 90:
6        print("Grade: B")
7    elif score >= 70 and score < 80:
8        print("Grade: C")
9    elif score >= 60 and score < 70:
10       print("Grade: D")
11   else:
12       print("Grade: F")
```

py grade.py

Score:78

Grade: C

Another version of **grade.py**

```
1    score = int(input("Score:"))
2
3    if 90 <= score <= 100:
4        print("Grade: A")
5    elif 80 <= score < 90:
6        print("Grade: B")
7    elif 70 <= score < 80:
8        print("Grade: C")
9    elif 60 <= score < 70:
10       print("Grade: D")
11   else:
12       print("Grade: F")
```

py grade.py

Score:78

Grade: C

A last one of grade.py

```
1    score = int(input("Score:"))
2
3    if score >= 90 :
4        print("Grade: A")
5    elif score >= 80 :
6        print("Grade: B")
7    elif score >= 70 :
8        print("Grade: C")
9    elif score >= 60 :
10       print("Grade: D")
11   else:
12       print("Grade: F")
```

py grade.py

Score:82

Now, we are going to check if a number is even or odd

The reminder is 0 or not.

Open a new file: **code even.py**

```
1    x = int(input("what's x?"))
2    if x % 2 == 0 :
3        print("Even")
4    else:
5        print("Odd")
```

py even.py

what's x?8
Even

Now, we are going to include this code in a function:

```
1    def main():
2        x = int(input("what's x?"))
3        if is_even(x): #passing on x
4            print("Even")
5        else:
6            print("Odd")
7
8    def is_even(n):
9        if n % 2 == 0 :
10           return True
11       else:
12           return False
13
14   main()
```

py even.py

what's x?7
Odd

Let's create a new file: house.py

In the terminal we enter: **code house.py**

```
1    name = input("what's your name?")
2    if name == "Yanis":
3        print("Bercy")
4    elif name == "Eric":
5        print("Bercy")
6    elif name == "Peter":
7        print("Queens")
8    else :
9        print("who?")
```

py house.py

what's your name?Yanis

Bercy

Note: when you run in your terminal "py.house.py", this command is to test your code.

What's your name? and I type "Yanis" but this time with a space between the question mark and Yanis, my code will skip to the line 9 and ask me "who?". To avoid this, we can add the function "strip()"

If we want the strip() function for all the names:

```
1    name = input("What's your name?").strip()
2
3    if name == "Yanis":
4        print("Bercy")
5    elif name == "Eric":
6        print("Bercy")
7    elif name == "Peter":
8        print("Queens")
9    else :
10       print("who?")
```

But if we want the **strip()** function to remove white spaces only for Yanis:

```
1    name = input("what's your name?")
2    if name.strip() == "Yanis":
3        print("Bercy")
4    elif name == "Eric":
5        print("Bercy")
6    elif name == "Peter":
7        print("Queens")
8    else :
9        print("who?")
```

Another version of **house.py**

```
1    name = input("what's your name?")
2
3    if name == "Yanis" or name == "Eric":
4        print("Bercy")
5    elif name == "Peter":
6        print("Queens")
7    else:
8        print("who?")
```

Another version:

Our code is using Python's new **match** statement introduced in Python 3.10. This is a great way to simplify conditional logic, especially when dealing with multiple conditions.

```
1    name = input("What's your name?")
2
3    match name:
4        case "Yanis":
5            print("Bercy")
6        case "Eric":
7            print("Bercy")
8        case "Peter":
9            print("Queens")
10       case _ :
11           print("Who?")

py house.py
what's your name?Peter
Queens
```

We can also do it this way

```
1    name = input("What's your name?")
2
3    match name:
4        case "Yanis" | "Eric" :
5            print("Bercy")
6        case "Peter":
7            print("Queens")
8        case _ :
9            print("Who?")
```

LOOPS

Let's go for a new python file.

code laugh.py

Let's say we want to code this in an other way:

print("haha")

print("haha")

print("haha")

So we want to represent someone who's laughing three times

Version 1

```
1    i = 3 # we initialize i
2
3    while i != 0:     # while i is not equal to 0
4        print("haha") # We print haha
5
6        i = i - 1     # after printing haha the first time, now i = 2
```

py laugh.py

haha
haha
haha

Always pay attention not to run an infinite loop. If you did so, to get out of that, you tape ; CTRL + C in the terminal

Version 2:

```
1   i = 1 # we initialize i
2
3   while i <= 3:    # while i is inferior or equal 3
4       print("haha") # We print haha
5
6       i = i + 1     # after printing haha the first time,  now i = 2
```

py laugh.py

haha
haha
haha

Version 3:

```
1   i = 0 # we initialize i
2
3   while i < 3:    # while i is inferior equal to 3
4       print("haha") # We print haha
5
6       i = i + 1     # after printing haha the first time now i = 1
7
```

py laugh.py

haha

haha

haha

Version 4

```
1    i = 0 # we initialize i
2
3    while i < 3:    # while i is inferior equal to 3
4        print("haha") # We print haha
5
6        i += 1      # after printing haha the first time now i = 1
7
```

py laugh.py

haha
```

## Version 5

```
1    for i in [0, 1, 2]:
2        print("haha")
```

py laugh.py

haha

haha

haha

Version 6

```
1    for i in range(3):
2        print("haha")
```

py laugh.py

haha

haha

haha
```

Version 7:

```
1    for _ in range(3):
2        print("haha")
```

py laugh.py

haha

haha

haha

Version 8:

```
1    print("haha\n" * 3)
```

py laugh.py

haha

haha

haha

In this version, if my script was only :

```
1    print("haha" * 3)
```

The output would have been:

hahahahahaha

Version 9:

```
print("haha\n"*3, end="")
```

py laugh.py

haha

haha

haha

Let the user choose the number of "haha" to display

```
1    n = int(input("What's n?"))
2
3    if n>0:
4        n = int(input("What's n?"))
5        if n<0:
6            n=...
```

We can do this code more efficiently

```
1  ∨ while True:
2        n = int(input("What's n?"))
3  ∨     if n<0:
4            continue
5  ∨     else:
6            break
```

py laugh.py

Try to test

```
1    while True:
2        n = int(input("What's n?"))
3        if n>0:
4            break
5    for i in range(n): # or for _ in range(n)
6        print("haha")
```

py laugh.py

What's n?4

haha
haha
haha
haha
```
```

Now let's try to use a function for our code:

```
1  def main():
2  |    haha(3)
3
4  def haha(n):
5       for _ in range(n):
6            print("haha")
7  main()
```

py laugh.py
haha
haha
haha

Another version :

First we define a **main()** function in which we need the n number for our "haha" function.

In "get_number", we extract the number of times we need to display "haha" in the "haha function"

Then we define the "haha function",

38

```
 1 ∨ def main():
 2         number = get_number()
 3         haha(number)
 4
 5 ∨ def get_number():
 6 ∨     while True:
 7             n = int(input("What's n?"))
 8 ∨         if n > 0:
 9                 break # Use break to get out of the loop
10         return(n) # return n, so we can use it in the "haha" function.
11
12 ∨ def haha(n):
13 ∨     for _ in range(n):
14             print("haha")
15     main()
```

py laugh.py

What's n? 5
haha
haha
haha
haha
haha

When we encapsulate our code within a function, it allows us to structure our code and make it more readable. This is especially true when our code starts to have more and more lines

LISTS

A list is always in **[ ]**

In a list of objects the first index is "0", the second index is "1" , etc.

If you want to access the first element of this list : months = [January, February, March, April, May]

For the first element: months[0], for the fourth element (here April) : months[3]

months[0] = January. months[3] = April

Let open a new python file:

code **profiles.py**

Version 1:

```
1    students = ["Yanis", "Eric", "Peter"]
2    print(students[0])
3    print(students[1])
4    print(students[2])
```

py profiles.py

Yanis
Eric
Peter

Version 2:

```
1    students = ["Yanis", "Eric", "Peter"]
2    for student in students:
3    |    print(student)
```

py profiles.py

Yanis
Eric
Peter

Version 3

```
1   students = ["Yanis", "Eric", "Peter"]
2 ∨ for i in range (len(students)):
3 |     print(students[i])
```

py profiles.py

Yanis
Eric
Peter

Version 4: Given that first element of the list has "0" as index, we want to know the top three students

```
1   students = ["Yanis", "Eric", "Peter"]
2 ∨ for i in range (len(students)):
3 |     print(i+1, students[i])
```

py profiles.py

1 Yanis

2 Eric

3 Peter

len() function:

The len() function is a built-in function in Python that is used to return the length of an object. The object can be a string, list, tuple, dictionary, or any other sequence or collection in Python.

How it works:

1. For strings: It returns the number of characters in the string.
2. For lists, tuples, and other sequences: It returns the number of elements in the sequence.
3. For dictionaries: It returns the number of key-value pairs in the dictionary.

Here are some examples of how to use the len() function:

```python
1    # String
2    string = "Hello, World!"
3    print(len(string))   # Output: 13
4
5    # List
6    my_list = [1, 2, 3, 4, 5]
7    print(len(my_list))   # Output: 5
8
9    # Tuple
10   my_tuple = (10, 20, 30)
11   print(len(my_tuple))   # Output: 3
12
13   # Dictionary
14   my_dict = {'a': 1, 'b': 2, 'c': 3}
15   print(len(my_dict))   # Output: 3
```

In each of these examples, the len() function is used to determine the size or length of the object specified, whether it's a string, list, tuple, or dictionary.

DICTIONARY

Data structure that allows you to associate one value with another.

List: A set of multiple values:

Yanis	Eric	Terry	Peter
Bercy	Bercy	Bercy	Queens

Students = ["Yanis", "Eric", "Terry", "Peter"] -> Keys

Houses = ["Bercy", "Bercy", "Bercy", "Queens"] -> Values

```
students = {
"Yanis":  "Bercy",
"Eric":   "Bercy",
"Terry": "Bercy",
"Peter": "Queens"
}

print(students["Yanis"])
print(students["Eric"])
print(students["Terry"])
print(students["Peter"])

Now here is the output:
py profiles.py
Bercy
Bercy
Bercy
Queens
```

Let's use the loop.
When you use a "for" loop to iterate over the dictionary, it iterates over the keys.

43

```
1    students = {
2    "Yanis":  "Bercy",
3    "Eric"  :  "Bercy",
4    "Terry": "Bercy",
5    "Peter": "Queens"
6    }
7
8    for student in students:
9        print(student)
```

py profiles.py

Yanis
Eric
Terry
Peter

What if we want to display the name and the house associated.

sep= "," is here to separate with commas the student and his house, otherwise, there would only be a white space between the two.

```
1    students = {
2    "Yanis":  "Bercy",
3    "Eric"  :  "Bercy",
4    "Terry": "Bercy",
5    "Peter": "Queens"
6    }
7
8    for student in students:
9        print(student, students[student], sep=",")
```

py profiles.py

Yanis,Bercy
Eric,Bercy
Terry,Bercy
Peter,Queens

	name	house	patronus
0	Yanis	Bercy	The wolf
1	Eric	Bercy	October
2	Terry	Bercy	Big show
3	Peter	Queens	

We are going to create a dictionary in a list.

```
students = [
    {"name": "Yanis", "house": "Bercy", "patronus"
: "The wolf"},
    {"name": "Eric", "house": "Bercy", "patronus" :
"October"},
    {"name": "Terry", "house": "Bercy", "patronus"
: "Big Show"},
    {"name": "Peter", "house": "Queens"}
]
```

We want to access the names:

```
1    students = [
2        {"name": "Yanis", "house": "Bercy", "patronus" : "The wolf"},
3        {"name": "Eric", "house": "Bercy", "patronus" : "October"},
4        {"name": "Terry", "house": "Bercy", "patronus" : "Big Show"},
5        {"name": "Peter", "house": "Queens"}
6    ]
7
8    for student in students:
9        print(student["name"])
```

py profiles.py

Yanis
Eric
Terry
Peter

Now, name and house

```
1    students = [
2        {"name": "Yanis", "house": "Bercy", "patronus" : "The wolf"},
3        {"name": "Eric", "house": "Bercy", "patronus" : "October"},
4        {"name": "Terry", "house": "Bercy", "patronus" : "Big Show"},
5        {"name": "Peter", "house": "Queens"}
6    ]
7    for student in students:
8        print(student["name"], student["house"], sep=",")
```

py profiles.py

Yanis,Bercy
Eric,Bercy
Terry,Bercy
Peter,Queens

Let's define a function **main()** and another function
print_square(size) which prints a square made of hash symbols
(#). The main() function calls print_square(3) to print a 3x3
square.Open a new file: **code square.py**

```
1    def main():
2        print_square(3)
3
4    def print_square(size):
5        #for each row in square
6        for i in range(size):
7            #for each brick in row
8            for j in range (size):
9                #print brick
10               print("#", end= "")
11           print()
12   main()
```

py square.py

###
###
###

46

```
1   def print_square(size):
2       for i in range(size):
3           print("#" * size)
4   main()
```

```
1   def print_square(size):
2       for i in range(size):
3           print_row(size)
4
5   def print_row(width):
6       print("#" * width)
7
8   main()
```

Don't know yet what prin_row(size) is, but you use it anyway in this function

EXCEPTIONS

Let's create a new file: code **exception.py**

```
1    x = int(input("what's x?"))
2    print(f"x is {x}")
```

If x is str for instance x = abc,
It will raise an error
ValueError: invalid literal for int() with base 10

We should code this way:

```
1    try:
2        x = int(input("what's x?"))
3        print(f"x is {x}")
4    except ValueError:
5        print("x is not an integer")
```

py exception.py

what's x?abc
x is not an integer

Or this way:

```
1    try:
2        x = int(input("what's x?"))
3    except ValueError:
4        print("x is not an integer")
5    else:
6        print(f"x is {x}")
```

py exception.py

what's x?5
x is 5

Another version:

```
1   while True:
2       try:
3           x = int(input("What's x?"))
4       except ValueError:
5           print("x is not an integer")
6       else:
7           break
8   print(f"x is {x}")
```

py exception.py

what's x?5
x is 5

If I didn't "break" and replaced it by "print(f"x is {x}), the program would still ask me what's x?

Now the final function in a main() function:

```
1   def main():
2       x = get_int()
3       print(f"x is {x}")
4
5   def get_int():
6
7       while True:
8           try:
9               x = int(input("What's x?"))
10          except ValueError:
11              print("x is not an integer")
12          else:
13              break
14      return x
15
16  main()
```

py exception.py

what's x?5

x is 5

49

"return", returns a value and breaks you out of a loop.

We can do this way:

```
1    def main():
2        x = get_int()
3        print(f"x is {x}")
4
5    def get_int():
6
7        while True:
8            try:
9                return int(input("What's x?"))
10           except ValueError:
11               print("x is not an integer")
12
13   main()
```

py exception.py
what's x?5
x is 5

PASS :

Until I don't specify a number, it will continue to ask me "What's x?"

```
1    def main():
2        x = get_int("What's x?")
3        print(f"x is {x}")
4
5    def get_int(prompt):
6
7        while True:
8            try:
9                return int(input(prompt))
10           except ValueError:
11               pass
12
13   main()
```

py exception.py
What's x?d
What's x?a
What's x?d
What's x?5

LIBRARIES

MODULES

docs.python.org/3/library/random.html

random function

Now we will learn how to use functions that have been already created by someone else.

You should know that python is an open source programing language, so everyone can contribute

What you should do to use the **random** function is to import it into your code editor:

Import random

coin = random.choice(["heads", "tails"])

print(coin)

This will display randomly "heads" or "tails" with the same probability.

Given that what we need is "choice" from random, what we can do is this:

from random import choice

coin = choice(["heads", "tails"])

print(coin)

Let's try another module:

```
1    import random
2
3    number = random.randint(1,10)
4    print(number)
```

51

Above, the output is 6, but could also be 5, 9, 7 …

In general, random.randint(a,b) gives you a random number between a and b inclusive

Random.shuffle(x). In the example below, outputs are: As, ten, queen, four

```
1    import random
2
3    cards = ["four", "ten", "As", "queen"]
4    random.shuffle(cards)
5    for card in cards:
6        print(card)
```

Statistics

docs.python.org/3/library/statistics.html

To use statistics, you also need to import the library
import statistics
print(statistics.mean([84,122]))

Command line arguments

docs.python.org/3/library/sys.html

Knowing how to use terminal commands is vital for a programmer.

Now we will learn some command line arguments in python.

sys.argv

In Python, **sys.argv** is a list that contains the command-line arguments passed to a Python script. The sys.argv list is part of the sys module, which provides access to some variables used or maintained by the Python interpreter, as well as functions that interact strongly with the interpreter.

Here's a breakdown of how sys.argv works:

sys.argv[0] is the name of the script being executed.

- ➔ If the Python script is being run directly, sys.argv[0] will be the script's filename.
- ➔ If the script is imported as a module, sys.argv[0] will be the name of the module.

sys.argv[1], sys.argv[2], and so on, contain the command-line arguments passed to the script. These arguments are separated by spaces when the script is executed from the command line.

For example, consider a Python script called example.py:

```
1    import sys
2
3    def main():
4        print("Script name:", sys.argv[0])
5        if len(sys.argv) > 1:
6            print("Arguments:", sys.argv[1:])
7        else:
8            print("No arguments provided.")
9
10   if __name__ == "__main__":
11   |   main()
12
```

If you run the script from the command line like this:

python example.py arg1 arg2 arg3

The output will be:

Script name: example.py

Arguments: ['arg1', 'arg2', 'arg3']

All right, maybe I've gone too fast. Let's take it slowly

sys.argv is an argument vector.

Suppose I edit this script in Vs code

File name: **example.py**

```
1    import sys
2
3    print("hello, my name is", sys.argv[1])
```

Now I want to interpret it from the command line:

python example.py Eric (here, the python file is "example.py" and Eric is an argument added)

The output will be: hello, my name is Eric

54

Now I think you start to understand.

In this example, if I don't give any argument, this message of exception will be displayed

```
1    import sys
2
3    try:
4        print("hello, my name is", sys.argv[1])
5    except IndexError:
6        print("Too few arguments")
```

python example.py

Too few arguments

In case we have too many or few arguments:

If no arguments: Too few arguments, if more than one argument: Too many arguments

```
1    import sys
2
3    if len(sys.argv) < 2 :
4        print("Too few arguments")
5    elif len(sys.argv) > 2:
6        print("Too many arguments")
7    else:
8        print("hello, my name is", sys.argv[1])
```

If there is no argument, the program stops.

```
1    import sys
2
3    if len(sys.argv) < 2:
4        sys.exit("Too few arguments")
5
6    for arg in sys.argv[1:]:
7        print("hello, my name is", arg)
```

PACKAGES: A third-party library to install

In Python, a package is a way of organizing related Python modules. A package can contain one or more modules, and it typically consists of a directory with a special file called: "init__.py".

Packages are used to organize and structure Python code into manageable units, making it easier to develop, maintain, and share Python projects and libraries. Python's package management system, including tools like **pip** and package indexes like **PyPI** (Python Package Index), further facilitates the distribution and installation of Python packages.

pypi.org

Example with cowsay

pypi.org/project/cowsay

To install, this can be done automatically within your terminal

pip install cowsay

Let's open a new file: code my_cowsay.py (Don't name your file "cowsay.py" there would be a conflict between your module and the name of your file, if you use that cowsay module)

```
1    import cowsay
2    import sys
3
4    if len(sys.argv) == 2 :
5    │    cowsay.cow("hello, " + sys.argv[1])
```

The code expects only one argument:

python my_cowsay.py World

output:

```
| hello, World |
  ============
              \
               \
                ^__^
               (oo)_____
               (__)\       )\/\
                   ||----w |
                   ||     ||
```

You can try to change "cowsay.cow" in "cowsay.trex" to see what changes.
```
```

REQUESTS

Requests:

pypi.org/project/requests

Requests is a simple, yet elegant, HTTP library.

Start by installing: **pip install requests** and giving a name to our file **(e.g request_file.py)**

```python
1   import requests
2   import sys
3
4   #errorchecking
5   if len(sys.argv) != 2:
6       sys.exit()
7
8   response = requests.get("https://itunes.apple.com/search?entity=song&limit=1&term=" + sys.argv[1])
9
10  print(response.json())
```

You can copie/paste this argument to avoid errors: ("https://itunes.apple.com/search?entity=song&limit =1&term=" + sys.argv[1])

How do we run our file request_file.py?

Our command line expects two arguments (the name of the file which is request_file.py and another one, the name of the band.

For instance, if the name of the band is "**Eric**":

 python request_file.py Eric (The following line is just the output; you don't have to read it)

58

{'resultCount': 1, 'results': [{'wrapperType': 'track', 'kind': 'song', 'artistId': 23224851, 'collectionId': 507287467, 'trackId': 507287635, 'artistName': 'Guthrie Govan', 'collectionName': 'Erotic Cakes', 'trackName': 'Eric', 'collectionCensoredName': 'Erotic Cakes', 'trackCensoredName': 'Eric', 'artistViewUrl': 'https://music.apple.com/us/artist/guthrie-govan/23224851?uo=4', 'collectionViewUrl': 'https://music.apple.com/us/album/eric/507287467?i=507287635&uo=4', 'trackViewUrl': 'https://music.apple.com/us/album/eric/507287467?i=507287635&uo=4', 'previewUrl': 'https://audio-ssl.itunes.apple.com/itunes-assets/AudioPreview126/v4/f6/cb/e9/f6cbe930-8028-ccd9-6984-f982c4ce356d/mzaf_4667918117532009017.plus.aac.p.m4a', 'artworkUrl30': 'https://is1-ssl.mzstatic.com/image/thumb/Music116/v4/fe/86/93/fe869354-5965-9548-7986-cc3e87fd132f/5037454798776_cover.jpg/30x30bb.jpg', 'artworkUrl60': 'https://is1-ssl.mzstatic.com/image/thumb/Music116/v4/fe/86/93/fe869354-5965-9548-7986-cc3e87fd132f/5037454798776_cover.jpg/60x60bb.jpg', 'artworkUrl100': 'https://is1-ssl.mzstatic.com/image/thumb/Music116/v4/fe/86/93/fe869354-5965-9548-7986-cc3e87fd132f/5037454798776_cover.jpg/100x100bb.jpg', 'collectionPrice': 9.99, 'trackPrice': 0.99, 'releaseDate': '2006-01-01T12:00:00Z', 'collectionExplicitness': 'notExplicit', 'trackExplicitness': 'notExplicit', 'discCount': 1, 'discNumber': 1, 'trackCount': 11, 'trackNumber': 8, 'trackTimeMillis': 305499, 'country': 'USA', 'currency': 'USD', 'primaryGenreName': 'Rock', 'isStreamable': True}]}

If the name of the band is "**sdsfefegf**"

```
$ python request_file.py sdsfefegf
```

{'resultCount': 0, 'results': []}

Let's do it differently:

```
1    import json
2    import requests
3    import sys
4
5    #errorchecking
6    if len(sys.argv) != 2:
7        sys.exit()
8
9    response = requests.get
10   ("https://itunes.apple.com/search?entity=song&limit=1&term=" + sys.argv[1])
11
12   print(json.dumps(response.json(), indent=2))
```

When we run our code:

$ python request_file.py Eric

{

 "resultCount": 1,

 "results": [

  {

    "wrapperType": "track",

    "kind": "song",

    "artistId": 23224851,

    "collectionId": 507287467,

    "trackId": 507287635,

"artistName": "Guthrie Govan",

"collectionName": "Erotic Cakes",

"trackName": "Eric",

"collectionCensoredName": "Erotic Cakes",

"trackCensoredName": "Eric",

"artistViewUrl": "https://music.apple.com/us/artist/guthrie-govan/23224851?uo=4",

"collectionViewUrl": "https://music.apple.com/us/album/eric/507287467?i=507287635&uo=4",

"trackViewUrl": "https://music.apple.com/us/album/eric/507287467?i=507287635&uo=4",

"previewUrl": "https://audio-ssl.itunes.apple.com/itunes-assets/AudioPreview126/v4/f6/cb/e9/f6cbe930-8028-ccd9-6984-f982c4ce356d/mzaf_4667918117532009017.plus.aac.p.m4a",

"artworkUrl30": "https://is1-ssl.mzstatic.com/image/thumb/Music116/v4/fe/86/93/fe869354-5965-9548-7986-cc3e87fd132f/5037454798776_cover.jpg/30x30bb.jpg",

"artworkUrl60": "https://is1-ssl.mzstatic.com/image/thumb/Music116/v4/fe/86/93/fe869354-5965-9548-7986-cc3e87fd132f/5037454798776_cover.jpg/60x60bb.jpg",

"artworkUrl100": "https://is1-ssl.mzstatic.com/image/thumb/Music116/v4/fe/86/93/fe869354-5965-9548-7986-cc3e87fd132f/5037454798776_cover.jpg/100x100bb.jpg",

"collectionPrice": 9.99,

```json
    "trackPrice": 0.99,

    "releaseDate": "2006-01-01T12:00:00Z",

    "collectionExplicitness": "notExplicit",

    "trackExplicitness": "notExplicit",

    "discCount": 1,

    "discNumber": 1,

    "trackCount": 11,

    "trackNumber": 8,

    "trackTimeMillis": 305499,

    "country": "USA",

    "currency": "USD",

    "primaryGenreName": "Rock",

    "isStreamable": true
  }
 ]
}
```

We are going to extract a trackName from an artist.

```
1    import json
2    import requests
3    import sys
4
5    #errorchecking
6    if len(sys.argv) != 2:
7        sys.exit()
8
9    response = requests.get
10   ("https://itunes.apple.com/search?entity=song&limit=1&term=" + sys.argv[1]
11
12   print(json.dumps(response.json(), indent=2))
13
14   o = response.json()
15   for result in o["result"]:
16       print(result["trackName"])
```

Let's run it from the terminal:

python request_file.py Kelly

Not My Daddy (feat. Stokley)

python request_file.py Michael

Man In the Mirror.

Let's open a new file: **sayings.py**

```
1    def main():
2        hello("world")
3        goodbye("world")
4
5    def hello(name):
6        print(f"hello, {name}")
7
8    def goodbye(name):
9        print(f"goodbye, {name}")
10
11   main()
```

python sayings.py

hello, world

goodbye, world

Let's open a new file: **greetings.py**

In the file **sayings.py** we created functions that we are going to use in our file **greetings.py**

```
1    import sys
2    from sayings import hello
3
4    if len(sys.argv)==2:
5        hello(sys.argv[1])
```
greetings.py

python greetings.py Eric

hello, world

goodbye, world

hello, Eric

64

main() in **sayings.py** is called. So, in **"sayings.py"** we should add this line at the end before **main():**

```
If __name__ == « __main__ » :

        main()
```

```
1    def main():
2        hello("world")
3        goodbye("world")
4
5    def hello(name):
6        print(f"hello,  {name}")
7
8    def goodbye(name):
9        print(f"goodbye, {name}")
10
11   if __name__ == "__main__":
12
13       main()
                                    sayings.py
```

Now, after modifying "sayings.py", try to run again "greetings.py" always from the command line.

Do you see the difference?

UNIT TEST

UNIT TEST

In Python, unit tests are a type of software testing where individual units or components of a program are tested in isolation. The purpose of unit testing is to validate that each unit of the software performs as designed.

Let's open a new file: **code calculator.py**

```
1    def main():
2        x = int(input("What's x?"))
3        print("x squared is", square(x))
4
5    def square(n):
6        return n*n
7
8    if __name__ == "__main__":
9        main()
```

py calculator.py

What's x?44

x squared is 1936

We can add error handling to our code using a **try-except** block to catch the **valueError** and prompt the user to enter a valid integer.

```
1    def main():
2        while True:
3            try:
4                x = int(input("What's x?"))
5                break   # Break out of the loop if input is valid
6            except ValueError:
7                print("Please enter a valid integer.")
8
9        print("x squared is", square(x))
10
11   def square(n):
12       return n * n
13
14   if __name__ == "__main__":
15       main()
```

py calculator.py

What's x?s

Please enter a valid integer.

What's x?-2

Now, let's open a new file for testing.

code test_calculator.py

Don't forget to import the function "**square()**" created in your calculator.py file

This test is quite simple. If we run the file **test_calculator.py** from the terminal, nothing is going to happen, simply because there is no error in our code.

```
1    from calculator import square
2
3    def main():
4        test_square()
5
6    def test_square():
7        if square(2) != 4:
8            print("2 squared was not 4")
9        if square(3) != 9:
10           print("3 squared was not 9")
11
12   if __name__ == "__main__":
13       main()
```

67

But If we change the file **calculator.py**, and we intentionally introduce an error into the 'square(n)' function?

We will change this line

def square(n):

    return n+n

```
1    def main():
2        while True:
3            try:
4                x = int(input("What's x?"))
5                break  # Break out of the loop if input is valid
6            except ValueError:
7                print("Please enter a valid integer.")
8
9        print("x squared is", square(x))
10
11   def square(n):
12       return n + n # we intentionally change n*n into n+n
13
14   if __name__ == "__main__":
15       main()
```

So, we will see the changes in **test_calculator.py**

```
1    from calculator import square
2
3    def main():
4        test_square()
5
6    def test_square():
7        if square(2) != 4:
8            print("2 squared was not 4")
9        if square(3) != 9:
10           print("3 squared was not 9")
11
12   if __name__ == "__main__":
13       main()
```

py test_calculator.py
python test_calculator.py
3 squared was not 9

3+3 = 6, It doesn't pass the test.

But 2+2 = 4 passes the square test just because 2*2 = 4

The **assert** keyword:

The **assert** keyword in Python is used as a debugging aid. It checks a condition, and if the condition is false, it raises an **AssertionError** exception with an optional error message.

The syntax for assert statement is:

```
assert condition, message
```

Here, **condition** is the expression that is being tested, and **message** is an optional string that can provide additional information about the assertion.

If the condition evaluates to **False**, the **assert** statement raises an **AssertionError** exception. If the condition evaluates to **True**, the program continues executing without any interruption.

```
x = 10

assert x == 5, "x is not equal to 5"
```

In this example, if **x** is not equal to **5**, the assert statement will raise an AssertionError with the message "**x** is not equal to **5**". If x is equal to 5, the program will continue executing as usual.

The assert statement is commonly used in unit testing to verify that the code behaves as expected. It helps developers catch bugs early in the development process.

Remember for tests purposes we've changed in **calculator.py** file, n*n to n+n.

Let's modify the test_calculator.py file:

```
1    from calculator import square
2
3    def main():
4        test_square()
5
6    def test_square():
7        assert square(2) == 4
8        assert square(3) == 9
9
10   if __name__ == "__main__":
11       main()
```

python test_calculator.py

Traceback (most recent call last):

 File "test_calculator.py", line 11, in <module>

  main()

 File "test_calculator.py", line 4, in main

  test_square()

 File "test_calculator.py", line 8, in test_square

  assert square(3) == 9

AssertionError

Assertion Error:

We've added other tests in test_calculator.py

Let's see the o

```
1   from calculator import square
2
3   def main():
4       test_square()
5
6   def test_square():
7       try:
8           assert square(2) == 4
9       except AssertionError:
10          print("2 squared was not 4")
11      try:
12          assert square(3) == 9
13      except AssertionError:
14          print("3 squared was not 9")
15  # We can add other tests
16      try:
17          assert square(-2) == 4
18      except AssertionError:
19          print("-2 squared was not 4")
20      try:
21          assert square(-3) == 9
22      except AssertionError:
23          print("-3 squared was not 9")
```

71

PYTEST

Pytest

What is Pytest?

First, let's install

pip install pytest

Pytest is a testing framework for Python that makes it easy to write simple and scalable test cases. It allows you to write tests in a more concise and readable way compared to the built-in **unittest** module.

Let's modify **test_calculator.py**

I invite you to run in terminal: pytest test_calculator.py

```
1    from calculator import square
2
3    def test_square():
4        assert square(2) == 4
5        assert square(3) == 9
6        assert square(-2) == 4
7        assert square(-3) == 9
8        assert square(0) == 0

pytest test_calculator.py
```

Here is another test

```
1    from calculator import square
2
3    def test_positive():
4        assert square(2) == 4
5        assert square(3) == 9
6
7    def test_negative():
8        assert square(-2) == 4
9        assert square(-3) == 9
```
pytest test_calculator.py

We can add a test:

```
1    from calculator import square
2    import pytest
3
4    def test_str():
5        with pytest.raises(TypeError):
6            square("cat")
```

Let's open a new file **code hello.py**

```
1    def main():
2        name = input("What's your name?")
3        hello(name)
4
5    def hello(to="World"):
6        print("hello, ",to)
7        #hello() prints something but
8        #doesn't return anything
9
10   if __name__ == '__main':
11       main()
```
python hello.py

Let's modify this file:

```
1    def main():
2        name = input("What's your name?")
3        hello(name)
4
5    def hello(to="World"):
6        return f"hello, {to}" # I'm returning hello, but not printing
7
8    if __name__ == "__main__":
9        main()
```

python hello.py

Now open a new test file: **code test_hello.py**

```
1    from hello import hello
2
3    def test_default():
4        assert hello() == "hello, world"
5
6    def test_argument():
7        assert hello("Eric") == "hello, Eric"
```

python test_hello.py

We can add a list of names in the test

```
1    from hello import hello
2
3    def test_default():
4        assert hello() == "hello, world"
5
6    def test_argument():
7        for name in ["Yanis", "Eric", "Terry", "Peter"]:
8            assert hello("name") == f"hello, {name}"
```

python test_hello.py

74

Let's create a new folder for test:

From terminal: type the following command

mkdir test (here we created a new folder named "test")

code test/test_hello.py (here, in the folder "test", there is a new file named "test_hello")

```
1    from hello import hello
2    def test_default():
3        assert hello() == "hello, world"
4
5    def test_argument():
6        assert hello("Eric") == "hello, Eric"
```

code test/__init__.py (This tells python to treat that folder as package)

Now to make sure we are still in the main directory in our pc

To see the current directory from the terminal, we must enter this command: **pwd**

To navigate up the directory tree from the current directory, you need to enter the following command from the terminal: **cd ..**

append() function

append () function.

The **append( )** function in Python is a method used specifically with lists. It is used to add an element to the end of a list. When you call **append( )** on a list, it modifies the original list by adding the specified element as its last element.

The syntax for **append( )**:

```
list_name.append(element)
```

• list_name is the name of the list to which you want to add an element.

• element is the value that you want to add to the end of the list.

Example:

```
my_list = [1, 2, 3]

my_list.append(4)

print(my_list)

# Output: [1, 2, 3, 4]
```

sorted() function:

In Python, the **sorted()** function is used to sort elements of an **iterable** (such as lists, tuples, or strings) in ascending order. It returns a new sorted list without modifying the original iterable.

The syntax for the sorted() function

```
sorted(iterable, key=None, reverse=False)
```

- iterable: The iterable (e.g., list, tuple, string) that you want to sort.
- key (optional): A function that specifies the sorting criterion. It takes one argument and returns a value to be used for sorting.
- reverse (optional): A boolean value that determines whether to sort the elements in descending order. By default, it's False (sorting in ascending order).

Examples:

Sorting a list:

```
numbers = [3, 1, 4, 1, 5, 9, 2, 6]
sorted_numbers = sorted(numbers)
print(sorted_numbers)
 # Output: [1, 1, 2, 3, 4, 5, 6, 9]
```

Sorting with custom key: here the key parameter is used to specify the sorting criterion. The list of students is sorted based on their ages.

```
students = [
    {"name": "Alice", "age": 25},
    {"name": "Bob", "age": 22},
    {"name": "Charlie", "age": 30}
]
sorted_students = sorted(students, key=lambda x:
x["age"])
print(sorted_students)

# Output: [{'name': 'Bob', 'age': 22}, {'name':
'Alice', 'age': 25}, {'name': 'Charlie', 'age':
```

Sorting a string.

```
text = "hello"
sorted_text = sorted(text)
print(sorted_text)
 # Output: ['e', 'h', 'l', 'l', 'o']
```

Let's open a new empty file: code **names.py**

```
1    names = []
2
3    for _ in range(3):
4        name = input("What's your name?")
5        names.append(name)
6    print(f"hello, {name}")
```

This code prompts the user to enter their name three times
and appends each name to the **names** list. Then, it prints
"hello, {name}" where {name} represents the last name
entered by the user. However, there's an issue with this code:
it prints the last name entered after the loop ends, which
might not be the intended behavior.

Let's make some modifications:

```
1    names = []
2
3    for _ in range(3):
4        names.append(input("What's your name? "))
5
6    for name in sorted(names):
7        print(f"Hello, {name}")
```

python names.py

What's your name? Emie
What's your name? Joseph
What's your name? Ronald
Hello, Emie
Hello, Joseph
Hello, Ronald

Let's add names in a new text file: **names.txt**

```
1    name = input("What's your name")
2    file = open("names.txt", "w")
3    file.write(name)
4    file.close()
5    #This code doesn't append every time
6    #But overwrites it.
7    #Now we need to fix it every time
8    #we add a name in the text file
9    #we'll have it shown
```

python names.py

What's your name?Seria

Open names.txt to check if "Seria" appears in your text file.

We made a little modification:

After modification, try to run the code from terminal as usual, three or four times and see what's going on, after entering three different names.

```
1    name = input("What's your name?")
2    file = open("names.txt", "a")
3    file.write(name)
4    file.close()
5    # Now it appends, but in a way we don't really like
```

python names.py

What's your name?Seria

python names.py

What's your name?Phil

python names.py

What's your name?Eric

Open now names.txt, you'll see the names appended are not the way we would like them to be.

Let's make some other modifications (modification of line 3)

```
1    name = input("What's your name?")
2    file = open("names.txt", "a")
3    file.write(f"{name}\n")
4    file.close()
```
python names.py

What's your name?Seria

THE WITH instruction

with:

In Python, the **with** statement is used to simplify the management of resources that need to be acquired and released properly, such as files, network connections, or database connections. It ensures that cleanup actions are performed automatically, even if exceptions occur during the execution of the code.

The with statement is commonly used with objects that support the context management protocol by implementing __enter__() and __exit__() methods.

Syntax for using with statement:

```
with expression as variable:
    # code block
```

expression is an object that supports the context management protocol.

variable is a variable to which the result of expression.__enter__() is assigned.

Within the "with" block, you can perform operations using the resource managed by the expression. When the block is exited, whether by normal execution or by an exception,

expression.__exit__() is called, allowing for proper cleanup.

Here's an example of using the with statement with file I/O to automatically close a file after its use:

```
with open("example.txt", "r") as file:
    content = file.read()
    print(content)
# At this point, the file is automatically
closed, even if an exception occurred while
```

In this example, the open() function returns a file object that supports the context management protocol. The "with" statement ensures that the file is properly closed after the block of code inside it is executed, regardless of whether an exception occurs or not.

"with": automatically opens and closes some files

```
1    name = input("What's your name?")
2    with open("names.txt", "a") as file:
3        file.write(f"{name}\n")
```

Now we are going are to read an existing file.
We will use the same file names.txt
Open this file and try to delete some names if you want.

```
1    with open("names.txt", "r") as file:
2        lines = file.readlines()
3    for line in lines:
4        print("hello", line)
```

python names.py

hello Peter
hello Georges
hello Tyra
hello emi

Another version.

Here we use, **rstrip()** function. It reduces the spaces between two lines.

```
1    with open("names.txt", "r") as file:
2
3        for line in file:
4            print("hello", line.rstrip())
```

python names.py

hello Peter
hello Georges
hello Tyra
hello emi

To sort the names, we read the file, we sort it, then print

```
1    names = []
2
3    with open("names.txt", "r") as file:
4
5        for line in file:
6            names.append(line.rstrip())
7        for name in sorted(names):
8            print(f"hello, {name}")
```

python names.py

hello Peter
hello Georges
hello Tyra
hello emi

Based on the output, it appears that the names are sorted alphabetically, but "emi" is sorted after "Tyra" instead of before it. This is because Python's default sorting behavior is case-sensitive, and lowercase letters are considered to have higher ASCII values than uppercase letters.

To sort the names in a case-insensitive manner, we can use the key parameter of the sorted() function and specify a function that converts each name to lowercase before sorting.

Here's how we can modify our code to achieve this:

```
1    names = []
2
3    with open("names.txt", "r") as file:
4        for line in file:
5            names.append(line.rstrip())
6
7    for name in sorted(names, key=lambda x: x.lower()):
8        print(f"hello, {name}")
```

py names.py

hello, emi
hello, Georges
hello, Peter
hello, Tyra

All this can be done more simply:

```
1    names = []
2
3    with open("names.txt", "r") as file:
4        for line in sorted(file, key=lambda x: x.lower()):
5            print("hello,", line.rstrip())
```

py names.py

Let's assume we may want to do some changes to the data (lower case, upper case, or other changes).

This has been done before in some other cases, and we also already know that we can use this function

sorted(iterable, /, *, key=None, reverse=False)

Now we had our file names.txt, we will transform it in name.csv

C.S.V. = Comma Separated Value

students.csv

1.Yanis
2.Bercy
3.Eric
4.Bercy
5.Terry
6.Bercy
7.Peter
8.Queens

Yanis, Bercy
Eric, Bercy
Terry, Bercy
Peter, Queens

We create students.csv and we create: students.py

```
1    with open("students.csv") as file:
2        for line in file:
3            row = line.rstrip().split(",")
4            print(f"{row[0]} is in {row[1]}")
```

py.students.py

Yanis is in Bercy
Eric is in Bercy
Terry is in Bercy
Peter is in Queens

The **split()** function on line 3 of our code splits each line of text from the file into a list of substrings based on a delimiter, which in this case is a comma (,).

A breakdown of how split() works in this context:

line.rstrip(): This removes any trailing whitespace characters, such as spaces or newline characters (\n), from the end of the line.

.split(","): This splits the resulting string into a list of substrings wherever a comma (,) is encountered. Each substring becomes an element of the list.

For example, if line is "Alice,Math", then line.rstrip().split(",") will produce the list ["Alice", "Math"].

In our code, each line of the file is assumed to contain two values separated by a comma, such as "Alice,Math". The split(",") function separates these two values into a list named row, and then row[0] and row[1] are used to access the first and second values, respectively, to print a message about the student and their course.

For the next lines, we can assign the row to name, house

Like this:

```
1    students = []
2
3    with open("students.csv") as file:
4        for line in file:
5            name, house = line.rstrip().split(",")
6            students.append(f"{name} is in {house}")
7
8    for student in sorted(students):
9        print(student)
```

py.students.py

Eric is in Bercy
Peter is in Queens
Terry is in Bercy
Yanis is in Bercy

Let's use dictionaries, but in this version, it is not sorted yet

```
1    students = []
2
3    with open("students.csv") as file:
4        for line in file:
5            name, house = line.rstrip().split(",")
6            student = {} #create an empty dictionary
7            student["name"] = name
8            student["house"] = house
9            students.append(student)
10
11   for student in students:
12       print(f"{student['name']} is in {student['house']}
```

py.students.py

Yanis is in Bercy
Eric is in Bercy
Terry is in Bercy
Peter is in Queens

87

To avoid conflicts, we use simple quotes in student['name'] and double quotes for f"

So, what if we add the sorted function?

```
1    students = []
2
3    with open("students.csv") as file:
4        for line in file:
5            name, house = line.rstrip().split(",")
6            student = {} #create an empty dictionary
7            student["name"] = name
8            student["house"] = house
9            students.append(student)
10
11   for student in sorted(students):
12       #Nothing is going to be sorted
13       #just by adding the sorted function
14       print(f"{student['name']} is in student{['house']}")
```

Traceback (most recent call last):

 File "students.py", line 11, in <module>

  for student in sorted(students):

TypeError: '<' not supported between instances of 'dict' and 'dict'

What we need to do is this:

We must tell python to sort the list by looking at the key in each dictionary, so it can sort either by name, or by house

```
1    students = []
2
3    with open("students.csv") as file:
4        for line in file:
5            name, house = line.rstrip().split(",")
6            student = {} #create an empty dictionary
7            student = {"name": name, "house": house}
8            students.append(student)
9
10   def get_name(student):
11       return student["name"]
12
13
14   for student in sorted(students, key = get_name):
15   |   print(f"{student['name']} is in {student['house']}")
```

python students.py
Eric is in Bercy
Peter is in Queens
Terry is in Bercy
Yanis is in Bercy

Here is the equivalence:

```
1    students = []
2
3    with open("students.csv") as file:
4        for line in file:
5            name, house = line.rstrip().split(",")
6            student = {} #create an empty dictionary
7            student = {"name": name, "house": house}
8            students.append(student)
9
10   for student in sorted(students, key = lambda student: student["name"]):
11   |   print(f"{student['name']} is in {student['house']}")
```

python students.py
Eric is in Bercy
Peter is in Queens
Terry is in Bercy

On line 10, in student: student["name"] for the first "student", I could call with any name, but I call it student because this function is passed in every single student in that list.

It might be xxxx:student["name"]

89

CSV FILES

CSV files.

docs.python.org/3/library/csv.html

import csv

```python
import csv

students = []

# Open the CSV file and read its content
with open("students.csv") as file:
    reader = csv.reader(file)
    next(reader)  # Skip the header, if present
    for row in reader:
        # Add each student to the list with the corresponding columns
        students.append({"name": row[0], "home": row[1]})

# Sort and display the students
for student in sorted(students, key=lambda student: student["name"]):
    print(f"{student['name']} is from {student['home']}")
```

python students.py

Eric is from Bercy
Peter is from Queens
Terry is from Bercy
Yanis is from Bercy

What if we replace : students.append({"name": row[0], "home": row[1]})" by

: students.append({"name": name, "home": home})

We'll have an error like this:

Traceback (most recent call last):

```
File "students.py", line 9, in <module>
    students.append({"name": name, "home": home})
NameError: name 'name' is not defined
```

Let's replace "reader" by "DictReader", which is going to give me automatic access to that column line.

But first in our csv file, we have to do some modification students.csv

1. name, home
2. Yanis, "River Plate, Roberto Street"
3. Eric, Sunset Beach
4. Terry, Melbourne Place
5. Peter, Down south

I'm using DictReader

```
1   import csv
2
3   students = []
4
5   with open("students.csv") as file:
6       reader = csv.DictReader(file)
7       for row in reader:
8           students.append({"name": row['name'], 'home': row['home']})
9
10  for student in sorted(students, key = lambda student: student['name']):
11      print(f"{student['name']} is from {student['home']}")
```

python students.py

Eric is from Sunset Beach
Peter is from Down South
Terry is from Melbourne Place
Yanis is from River Plate, Roberto Street

```
1    import csv
2
3    name = input("What's your name?")
4    home = input("Where's your home?")
5
6    # Now write instead of reading
7
8    with open("students.csv", "a") as file:
9        writer = csv.writer(file)
10       writer.writerow([name, home])
```

python students.py

What's your name?Yanis

Where's your home?River Plate, Roberto Street

Another way to implement the code is to use DictWriter, so we don't have to worry about the order.

```
1    import csv
2
3    name = input("What's your name?")
4    home = input("Where's your home?")
5
6    with open("students.csv", "a") as file:
7        writer = csv.DictWriter(file,fieldnames = ["name", "home"])
8        writer.writerow({"name":name, "home":home})
```

python students.py

What's your name?Eric
Where's your home?Sunset Beach

PILLOW LIBRARY

PILLOW LIBRARY:

Pillow is a Python Imaging Library (PIL) fork. It adds image processing capabilities to your Python interpreter, including:

Opening, manipulating, and saving many different images file formats.

Handling image metadata, such as Exif data.

Basic image editing operations, such as cropping, resizing, rotating, and flipping images.

Adding text and drawing shapes to images.

Applying various filters and effects to images.

Pillow is widely used for tasks such as image manipulation, processing, and generation in various Python applications, including web development, scientific computing, and image processing projects. It provides a comprehensive set of functionalities for working with images efficiently and effectively.

Let's assume we have a pet image in two different positions called **dog1.gif** and **dog2.gif**

Let's open a new python file called **dogs.py**

You can open gif files in Vs code :

code dog1.gif

code dog2.gif

Eventually, this going to create a new file after running our code
called **dogs.gif**

```
1   import sys
2
3   from PIL import Image
4
5   images = []
6   for arg in sys.argv[1:]:
7       image = Image.open(arg)
8       images.append(image)
9
10  images[0].save(
11      "dogs.gif", save_all = True, append_images = [images[1]], duration = 200, loop = 0
12      )
```

python dogs.py dog1.gif dog2.gif

REGULAR EXPRESSIONS

Library: re

Regular expressions, often abbreviated as regex or regexp

docs.python.org/3/library/re.html

Regular expressions are a versatile and powerful tool for text processing in Python, allowing you to perform complex pattern matching and manipulation tasks with ease. However, they can also be challenging to learn and understand, particularly for complex patterns.

Practice and experimentation are key to mastering regular expressions effectively.

Simple example with email:

```python
email = input("What's your email?").strip()
if "@" in email:
    print("valid")
else:
    print("Invalid")
```

Another example:

```python
email = input("What's your email?").strip()

username, domain = email.split("@")
if username:
    print("valid")
else:
    print("Invalid")
```

But for a valid email, we have so many points to watch to decide if it is valid or not (domain, what comes before "@" and after, etc.)

Some characters used in regular expressions

```
. any character except a new line
* 0 or more repetitions
+ 1 or more repetitions
? 0 or 1 repetition
{m} m repetitions
{m, n} m-n repetitions
```

We can open a new python file name "email.py"
code **email.py**

```
1    import re
2
3    email = input("What's your email?").strip()
4
5    username, domain = email.split("@")
6    if re.search(".+@.+", email):
7        print("valid")
8    else:
9        print("Invalid")
```

Here, the regular expression pattern ".+@.+" matches any string that contains at least one character before and after the "@" symbol

Let's assume this email address is valid: doe@country.gov

We may use this line if re.search(".+@.+.gov, email). We have to use an escape character (back slash) to tell python we want a new line.

96

```
1    import re
2
3    email = input("What's your email?").strip()
4
5    if re.search(r".+@.+\.gov", email):
6        print("valid")
7    else:
8        print("Invalid")
```

py email.py

What's your email?doe@country.gov

Valid

py email.py

What's your email?doe@country?gov

Invalid

py email.py

What's your email?doe@@@country.gov

valid

As we can see above, there is a problem for
"doe@@@country.gov" to be a valid email

So, How to be more precise?

We can add a "$" character.
```
if re.search(r".+@.+\.gov$", email):
```
This regular expression pattern ends with \.gov$. The $ symbol is a
metacharacter in regular expressions that matches the end of the
string. So, this pattern will match any string that ends with .gov

```
if re.search(r".+@.+\.gov", email):
```

This regular expression pattern does not end with **$**. Therefore, it will match any string that contains .gov anywhere in the string, not necessarily at the end.

The first expression will match email addresses ending with .gov, such as **example@gov**, **user@domain.gov**, etc.

The second will match any email address containing .gov anywhere in the string, including cases where .gov appears in the middle or at the end of the email address.

For example, it will match **example@gov**, **user@domain.gov**, **example.gov@example.com**, etc.

Depending on your specific requirements for matching email addresses, you would choose the appropriate regular expression pattern.

If you're specifically looking for email addresses with .gov at the end, you would use expression 1. If you want to match any email address containing .gov anywhere in the string, you would use expression 2.

But, to be even more precise, we have to add this character: ^

```
if re.search(r"^.+@.+\.gov$", email)
```
This regular expression pattern starts with ^ and ends with $. These symbols are metacharacters in regular expressions:

```
^: Matches the start of the string.
$: Matches the end of the string.
```

Note: "." Is not a special character but it is a symbol as it is, just a stop, and the "\" tells the computer to not treat the symbol as a special character.

So, this pattern will match any string that starts with one or more characters, followed by @, followed by one or more characters, followed by .gov, and finally ends at the end of the string.

In summary:

expression 3 will match email addresses that start with any characters, followed by @, followed by any characters, and ending with .gov. It ensures that the entire string consists of an email address ending with .gov.

For example, it will match **example@gov**, **user@domain.gov**, etc., but it will not match **example@gov.com** or **example.gov@example.com**.

But, "**doe@@@country.gov**" is still valid.

Let's see other characters:

[ ] set of characters. Defines character classes, allowing you to match any character within the specified set

Inside the square brackets, you list the characters you want to match.

For example:

  • [abc]: Matches any single character that is either 'a', 'b', or 'c'.

  • [a-zA-Z]: Matches any single alphabetic character, either lowercase or uppercase.

  • [0-9]: Matches any single digit character.

  • [aeiou]: Matches any single vowel character.

[1] refers to specific character groups captured by capturing groups in the regular expression pattern

1. You can also use ranges (-) and character classes within character classes. For example, [a-z0-9] matches any lowercase alphabetic character or digit.

2. [1]: Square brackets containing a number, such as [1], are used to reference a specific character group captured by a capturing group in the regular expression pattern.

> • For example, if you have a regular expression pattern with a capturing group (..), which captures any two characters, and you want to reference the first captured group, you would use [1].

> • Similarly, if you have multiple capturing groups, you can reference them using [2], [3], and so on, to refer to the corresponding captured groups.

For instance, if your pattern is (..)\d(.), and you're matching against the string "ab3c", [1] would refer to "ab" and [2] would refer to "c".

[^] The complement: which means anything except that character, the symbol you want to exclude

We could also do this way:

```
if re.search(r"^[^@]+@[^@]+\.gov$",
             email)
```

1.   ^: This metacharacter matches the start of the string.

2.   [^@]+: This part of the pattern matches one or more characters (+) that are not @ ([^@]). The ^ inside the square brackets negates the character class, meaning it matches any character except @. So, [^@]+ matches one or more characters before the @ symbol.

3.   @: This matches the @ symbol in the email address.

4.   **[^@]+**: This part matches one or more characters that are not @ ([^@]). It matches the domain part of the email address.

5.   **\.**: This matches a literal dot (.). The backslash \ is used to escape the dot, as . is a metacharacter in regular expressions and matches any character. We want to match a literal dot.

6.   **gov**: This matches the literal characters gov at the end of the string.

7.   **$**: This metacharacter matches the end of the string.

Can you tell what is the "r" in our expression?

In the expression re.search(r"^[^@]+@[^@]+\.gov$", email), the **r** prefix before the regular expression string indicates that it is a "raw string literal" in Python.

When you prefix a string literal with **r**, Python treats backslashes **** in the string as literal characters, rather than as escape characters. This means that backslashes are not used to escape special characters within the string.

For example, without the **r** prefix, you would need to write the regular expression pattern as "^[^@]+@[^@]+\\.gov$" to properly escape the dot . character. With the r prefix, you can write the pattern as r"^[^@]+@[^@]+\.gov$" and Python will treat the dot . as a literal character.

Using raw strings with regular expressions can make the patterns more readable and easier to understand, as you don't need to worry about double escaping characters that have special meaning in regular expressions.

In summary, the r prefix before the regular expression string indicates that it is a raw string

```
1   import re
2
3   email = input("What's your email?").strip()
4
5   if re.search(r"^[^@]+@[^@]+\.gov$", email):
6       print("valid")
7   else:
8       print("Invalid")
```

We can add other restrictions:

[a-z] : Define what we're going to tolerate in username. Only allow characters that appear in normal words: a, b, c, ... , z

[a-zA-Z]: Here, we include uppercase

[a-zA-Z0-9], we additionally we add numbers. If I want the restrictions to the right, I'll do the same, Copie/Paste

```
import re

email = input("What's your email?").strip()

if re.search(r"^[a-zA-Z0-9]+@[a-zA-Z0-9]+\.gov$", email):
    print("valid")
else:
    print("Invalid")
```

We can replace: [a-zA-Z0-9] by w

if re.search(r"^\w+@\w+\.gov$", email):

Note: "w" is in lowercase. If "W" is in uppercase this means it represents the negation of \w, meaning it matches any character that is not a word character.

Partial list:

\d : decimal digit

\D : not a decimal digit

\s : not a whitespace character

\w: word character...as well as numbers and underscore

\W: not a word character

A\B: either A or B

Why DOE@COUNTRY.GOV is invalid ?

It's because of the Uppercase.

```
if re.search(r"^\w+@\w+\.gov$", email.lower())
```

We have: re.IGNORECASE

        re.MULTILINE

        re.DOTALL

We can pass the third argument of re.search

```
import re

email = input("What's your email?").strip()

if re.search(r"^\w+@\w+\.gov$", email,
        re.IGNORECASE):
        print("valid")
    else:
```

```
print("Invalid")
```

We said that all things in the parenthesis can either be there once or be there not at all (0 times)

```
r"^\w+@(\w+\.)?\w+\.gov$", email, re.IGNORECASE
```

(\w+\.)? : The question mark means all things on parenthesis can be there or not.

If I remove the parenthesis, that means only "." can be there or not

For regular expression of a valid email, it is more complicated that it seems.

This is how browsers implement them:

Here is the regular expression for valid email address, how browsers implement them currently:

^[a-zA-Z0-9.!#$%&'*+\/=?^_`{|}~-]+@[a-zA-Z0-9]?:[a-zA-Z0-9-]{0,61}[a-zA-Z0-9] ?(?:\.[a-zA-Z0-9](?:[a-zA-Z0-9-]{0,61}[a-zA-Z0-9])?)?)

re.match

we have:

```
re.match(pattern, string, flags=0)
re.fullmatch(pattern, string, flags=0)
```

104

Let's open a new file: format.py

```
1    name = input("what's your name?").strip()
2    print(f"hello {name}")
```

py format.py

what's your name? Jackson, Peter

hello Jackson, Peter

What if you want to fix the first name before the last? We can use the "split()" function.

```
1    name = input("what's your name?").strip()
2    if "," in name:
3        last, first = name.split(",")
4        name = f"{first} {last}"
5
6    print(f"hello, {name}")
```

py format.py

what's your name?Jackson, Peter

hello, Peter Jackson

Despite this update, there might be a problem.

"split()" is supposed to split the strings into 2 strings looking for the comma and space, but what if there is no any of these?

I might make the space optional.

With the regular expression, we have the question mark symbol (?) means 0 or 1 things on the left.

In my problem, I must have a comma and may or may not have a space, 0 or 1 space

```
1    import re
2
3    name = input("what's your name?").strip()
4    matches = re.search(r"^(.+), (.+)$", name)
5    if matches:
6        last, first = matches.groups()
7        name = f"{first} {last}"
8
9    print(f"hello, {name}")
```

py format.py

what's your name?Peter Jackson
hello, Peter Jackson

Remember:

A|B : either A or B

(?:...) non-capturing Version

I want to get the user's last name, and the first name

(.+) I'm not adding a question mark, I'm using parenthesis for capturing purposes

Everything captured in "( )" will be returned to me as returned values

In the test above, I taped my name "Peter Jackson", but nothing happened with the "if condition" just because I did not type a comma

I can try this: It seems to still break

```
1    import re
2
3    name = input("what's your name?").strip()
4    matches = re.search(r"^(.+), (.+)$", name)
5    if matches:
6    |    name = matches.group(2)+" "+matches.group(1)
7    print(f"hello, {name}")
```

py format.py

what's your name?Jackson,Peter
hello, Jackson,Peter

A better version

```
1    import re
2
3    name = input("what's your name?").strip()
4    matches = re.search(r"^(.+), ?(.+)$", name)
5    if matches:
6    |    name = matches.group(2)+" "+matches.group(1)
7    print(f"hello, {name}")
```

py format.py

what's your name?Jackson, Peter
hello, Peter Jackson
what's your name?Jackson,   Peter
hello,   Peter Jackson

We see in the second test that there is a problem of white space to solve here.

If I have a space and a question mark, no need for parenthesis, then I can literally tolerate Jackson, Peter

```
1    import re
2
3    name = input("what's your name?").strip()
4    matches = re.search(r"^(.+), *(.+)$", name)
5    if matches:
6        name = matches.group(2)+" "+matches.group(1)
7    print(f"hello, {name}")
```

py format.py

what's your name?Jackson,   Peter

hello, Peter Jackson

We can use another symbol:

:= Assigns a value from right to left and ask a Boolean question about it

```
1    import re
2
3    name = input("what's your name?").strip()
4    if matches := re.search(r"^(.+), *(.+)$", name):
5        name = matches.group(2)+" "+matches.group(1)
6    print(f"hello, {name}")
```

group() function:

In Python's re module, the group() function is a method used to extract the substring that was matched by a specific capturing group within a regular expression pattern.

When you use parentheses () in a regular expression pattern, it creates a capturing group. Each capturing group captures a portion of the input string that matches the pattern enclosed within the parentheses.

After performing a search or match operation using **re.search**() or **re.match**(), you can use the **group()** method on the resulting match object to retrieve the substring that was captured by a specific capturing group.

Here's how you can use group()

```python
import re

text = "Hello, world!"
pattern = r"(\w+), (\w+)"

match = re.search(pattern, text)
if match:
    print("Full match:", match.group(0))  # Full match
    print("First capture group:", match.group(1))  # First capturing group
    print("Second capture group:", match.group(2))  # Second capturing group
```

In this example:

(\w+) captures the first word in the string.

, matches the comma and space.

(\w+) captures the second word in the string.

The group() method allows you to access the substrings captured by these groups.

match.group(0) returns the entire substring that matches the entire pattern, while match.group(1) and match.group(2) return the substrings captured by the first and second capturing groups, respectively.

You can also pass multiple group numbers to group() to access multiple capturing groups at once. For example, match.group(1, 2) would return a tuple containing the substrings captured by the first and second capturing groups.

Another example:

```python
import re

# Input string
text = "The price of apples is $2.50 and oranges is $3.00."

# Regular expression pattern to match prices
pattern = r"\$(\d+\.\d{2})"  # Capturing group
captures the price

# Search for prices in the text
matches = re.finditer(pattern, text)

# Iterate over matches
for match in matches:
```

```
    # Get the substring captured by the capturing
group
    price = match.group(1)
    print("Found price:", price)
```

In this example:

The input string contains information about the prices of apples and oranges.

The regular expression pattern r"\$(\d+\.\d{2})" is used to match the prices.

\$(\d+\.\d{2}) captures the price value, which consists of digits followed by a dot and two decimal places.

The finditer() function is used to search for all occurrences of the pattern in the text.

Inside the loop, **match.group(1)** is used to extract the substring captured by the capturing group. Since there is only one capturing group in the pattern, we use **group(1)** to access the substring.

When you run this code, it will output:

Found price: 2.50

Found price: 3.00

EXTRACTING INFORMATION

EXTRACTING INFORMATION:

code twitter.py

We would like to extract the information of a user's profile on twitter.

Open a new python file: code twitter.py

```
url   input("URL ").strip()
print(url)

Test: py twitter.py
URL: http://twitter.com/johndoe
```

So, in this case, how do I extract the user's name?

Just by ignoring everything in the beginning

```
url = input("URL: ").strip()
username = url.replace(https://twitter.com/, " ")
print(f"username:{username})

Test: py twitter.py
URL: http://twitter.com/johndoe
username: johndoe
```

Of course, this method has many drawbacks.

The start of the url could be: twitter.com, https... www.. etc.

Let's introduce: **re.sub()**

```
1   import re
2
3   url = input("URL: ").strip()
4   username = re.sub(r"https://twitter.com/","", url)
5   print(f"Username: {username}")
```

py twitter.py

URL: https://twitter.com/johndoe

Username: johndoe

There always be missing hypotheses.

We're going to modify our regular expression.

The next one is really hard to read if you are not the author. So you should go step by step.

You do something simple, and you see if it works or not. Avoid doing all in one step.

```
1   import re
2
3   url = input("URL: ").strip()
4   username = re.sub(r"(https?://)?(www\.)?twitter\.com/","", url)
5   print(f"Username: {username}")
```

What if we test: https://www.google.com/
Output would be: https://www.google.com/
This output does not satisfy us.

```
1   import re
2
3   url = input("URL: ").strip()
4   matches = re.search(r"^https?://(www\.)?twitter\.com/(.+)$",url,re.IGNORECASE)
5   if matches:
6
7       print(f"Username:", matches.group(1))
```

The same test, but now I have no Output

If I test "https://twitter.com/johndoe", I have this output: None.
If I test "https://www.twitter.com/johndoe", I have this output:
www.
The subdomain was not optional, to make it optional, let's change
group(1)->group(2)

```
1    import re
2
3    url = input("URL: ").strip()
4    matches = re.search(r"^https?://(www\.)?twitter\.com/(.+)$",url,re.IGNORECASE)
5    if matches:
6    |
7    |    print(f"Username:", matches.group(2))
```

With this change, If I test "https://www.twitter.com/johndoe", I
have this output: johndoe

Now we can insert :=

```
1    import re
2
3    url = input("URL: ").strip()
4    if matches:= re.search(r"^https?://(www\.)?twitter\.com/(.+)$",url,re.IGNORECASE):
5    |
6    |    print(f"Username:", matches.group(2))
```

We can change this (www\.) in this (?:www\.) and add a space ..,
url, re

```
1    import re
2
3    url = input("URL: ").strip()
4    if matches:= re.search(r"^https?://(?:www\.)?twitter\.com/(.+)$", url, re.IGNORECASE):
5    |
6    |    print(f"Username:", matches.group(1))
```

There are some other functions for regular expressions:

re.sub(pattern, repl, string,count=0, flags)

re.split , re.findallSo I invite you to practice and read
documentations

114

OBJECT ORIENTED PROGRAMING

OBJECT-ORIENTED-PROGRAMING (OOP)

Object-oriented programming (OOP) is a programming paradigm that revolves around the concept of "objects".

In OOP, software is structured as a collection of objects that interact with each other to perform tasks and solve problems.

These objects are instances of classes, which serve as blueprints for creating objects with similar characteristics and behaviors.

Let's open a new file: **code student.py**

```
1    def main():
2        name = input("Name: ")
3        house = input("House: ")
4        print(f"{name} from {house}")
5
6    main()
```

Now let's try to do it in a different way:

```
1    def main():
2        name = get_name() # We assume we have a function named "get_name"
3        house = get_house() # We assume we have a function named "get_house"
4        print(f"{name} from {house}")
5    # Now let's implement these functions
6
7    def get_name():
8        name = input("Name: ")
9        return name
10
11   def get_house():
12       return input("House: ")
13
14   if __name__ == "__main__":
15       main()
```

115

Version 3:

```
1    def main():
2        name, house = get_student()
3        print(f"{name} from {house}")
4
5    def get_student():
6        name = input("Name: ") # i could replace here name, house by n, h
7        house = input("House: ")
8        return name, house
9
10   if __name__ == "__main__":
11       main()
```

You can try to test by running **python student.py**

Let's talk about **Tuple**:

A *tuple* in Python is an immutable (unchangeable) collection of elements. It is similar to a list, but unlike lists, tuples cannot be modified after they are created. Tuples are defined using parentheses () and can contain elements of different data types separated by commas.

Example:

my_tuple = (1, 2, 3, 'hello', True)

In this example, my_tuple is a tuple containing integers, a string, and a boolean value.

Key features of tuples include:

Immutable: Once a tuple is created, its elements cannot be changed, added, or removed. This means that tuples provide a level of data integrity and safety, particularly when you want to ensure that certain data remains unchanged.

116

Ordered: Like lists, tuples are ordered collections, which means that the order of elements in a tuple is preserved. You can access elements in a tuple by their index.

Heterogeneous: Tuples can contain elements of different data types, allowing you to create tuples with a mix of integers, strings, floats, booleans, or even other tuples.

Indexing and Slicing: You can access individual elements in a tuple using square brackets and the index of the element. Tuples also support slicing, which allows you to extract a subset of elements from the tuple.

Example of accessing elements in a tuple:

```python
my_tuple = (1, 2, 3, 'hello', True)

print(my_tuple[0])   # Output: 1
print(my_tuple[3])   # Output: 'hello'
print(my_tuple[-1])  # Output: True
print(my_tuple[1:4]) # Output: (2, 3, 'hello')
```

Tuples are commonly used in Python for tasks such as returning multiple values from a function, representing fixed collections of data, and as keys in dictionaries (since they are immutable).

Let's modify our code by transforming in a tuple (name, house)

```python
1  def main():
2      name, house = get_student()
3      print(f"{name} from ,{house}")
4
5  def get_student():
6      name = input("Name: ") # i can replace name, house by n, h
7      house = input("House: ")
8      return (name, house) #<- we have a tuple
9
10 if __name__ == "__main__":
11     main()
```

We can add some conditions

```
1   def main():
2
3       student = get_student()
4       if student[0] == "Anna":
5           student[1] = "Svenska"
6       print(f"{student[0]} from {student[1]}")
7
8   def get_student():
9       name = input("Name: ")
10      house = input("House: ")
11      return (name, house) # <- here it's a tuple
12
13  if __name__ == "__main__":
14      main()
```

Let's try to test: **python student.py**

Name: Anna

House: Svenska

TypeError: 'tuple' object does not support item assignment

To avoid this error: We can change line 11 "return (name, house)"
in "return [name, house]

```
1   def main():
2
3       student = get_student()
4       if student[0] == "Anna":
5           student[1] = "Svenska"
6       print(f"{student[0]} from {student[1]}")
7
8   def get_student():
9       name = input("Name: ")
10      house = input("House: ")
11      return [name, house]
12
13  if __name__ == "__main__":
14      main()
```

Let's try some tests:

Name: Anna	Name: Anna
House: Brighton	House: Svenska
Output: Anna from Svenska	Output: Anna from Svenska

Now I want to access the key inside a dictionary not by numeric index which is for tuple and list, but the way of the keys.

You don't have to remember the index ... [0] is this... [1] is that...

```
1   def main():
2
3       student = get_student()
4       print(f"{student['name']} from {student['house']}")
5       #Attention to double quotes and single quote
6
7   def get_student():
8       student = {}
9       student["name"] = input("Name: ")
10      student["house"] = input("House: ")
11      return student
12
13  if __name__ == "__main__":
14      main()
```

We can modify the main function:

```
1   def main():
2
3       student = get_student()
4       if student["name"] == "Anna":
5           student["house"] = "Svenska"
6       print(f"{student['name']} from {student['house']}")
7
8   def get_student():
9       name = input("Name: ")
10      house = input("House: ")
11      return {"name": name, "house": house}
12
13  if __name__ == "__main__":
14      main()
```

119

CLASSES

CLASSES :

We have already defined what is a class in python in object-oriented programming (OOP).

What I can add is that class allows you to invent your data types in python and give them a name.

docs.python.org/3/tutorial/classes.html

Let's now just implement them:

```
1   class Student:
2       ... # for now we keep this space empty.
3
4
5   def main():
6
7       student = get_student()
8       print(f"{student.name} from {student.house}")
9
10  def get_student():
11      student = Student()
12      name = input("Name: ")
13      house = input("House: ")
14      return student
15
16  if __name__ == "__main__":
17      main()
```

By convention, class names are always in capital letters: class Name.

Anytime you use a class, you're creating what is called object.

120

On the line student = Student(), I'm creating an object of that class. A class is the definition of a new data type. The object is the instantiation of that class.

I have now a proper data type called "Student"

I can simplify my code:

```
1    def get_student():
2        name = input("Name: ")
3        house = input("House: ")
4        student = Student(name, house)
5        return student
```

Compared to previously:

```
1    def get_student():
2        student = Student()
3        student.name = input("Name: ")
4        student.house = input("House: ")
```

Methods
In object-oriented programming (OOP), methods are functions that are defined within a class and operate on objects of that class. They represent the behavior or actions that objects of the class can perform. Methods are associated with specific classes and are invoked on instances (objects) of those classes.

Key points :

Defined within a class: Methods are defined within the body of a class definition. They are declared using the def keyword, just like regular functions, but they are nested within the class definition.

Accessing object state: Methods have access to the attributes (state) of the object they belong to. They can read and modify the object's attributes using dot notation (self.attribute).

self parameter: The first parameter of a method is typically named self, which refers to the instance of the class on which the method is being called. Inside the method, self is used to access the attributes and other methods of the object.

Instance methods: Most commonly, methods in Python are instance methods, meaning they operate on individual instances (objects) of the class. When you call an instance method on an object, the object automatically becomes the self-parameter.

Behavior definition: Methods define the behavior of objects of the class. They encapsulate the operations that objects can perform, such as modifying their state, performing calculations, interacting with other objects, or providing information about themselves.

Modularity and organization: Methods provide a modular and organized way to structure code within a class. They group related behaviors together, making the class definition easier to understand and maintain.

Example :

```
1   class Dog:
2       def __init__(self, name, age):
3           self.name = name
4           self.age = age
5
6       def bark(self):
7           print(f"{self.name} says woof!")
```

In this example, **bark()** is a method of the **Dog class**. It defines the behavior of a Dog object by making it bark. When you call bark() on a Dog object, it prints a message indicating that the dog is barking

```
1   # Create a Dog object
2   my_dog = Dog("Buddy", 3)
3
4   # Call the bark() method on the Dog object
5   my_dog.bark()  # Output: "Buddy says woof!
```

Methods in Python are functions defined within a class that operate on objects of that class. They define the behavior of objects and provide a way to encapsulate related functionality within a class definition.

Let's return to our python file student.py

```python
class Student:
    def __init__(self, name, house):
        self.name = name
        self.house = house


def main():

    student = get_student()
    print(f"{student.name} from {student.house}")

def get_student():
    name = input("Name: ")
    house = input("House: ")
    student = Student(name, house)
    return student
```

The line: student = Student(name, house) is a constructor. It constructs an object. But initially, it is empty. No name, no house, but the object exists in the computer's memory.

__init__ method initializes the content of an object from a class. Then we add variables to objects

We could also do this : self.n = name

self.h = house

Object is just an instance of a class

What else can we do with classes? -> add return method

```
1    class Student:
2        def __init__(self, name, house):
3            if not name:
4                raise ValueError("Missing Name")
5            if house not in ["Queens", "Bercy", "Sunset Beach", "Brighton"]:
6                raise ValueError("Invalid house")
7            self.name = name
8            self.house = house
9
10   def main():
11       student = get_student()
12       print(f"{student.name} from {student.house}")
13
14   def get_student():
15       name = input("Name: ")
16       house = input("House: ")
17       student = Student(name, house)
18       return student
19
20   if __name__ == "__main__":
21       main()
```

Let's make a change and give to __init__ more arguments:

```
1    class Student:
2        def __init__(self, first, middle, last, house):
3            if not first:
4                raise ValueError("Missing Name")
5            if house not in ["Queens", "Bercy", "Sunset Beach", "Brighton"]:
6                raise ValueError("Invalid house")
7            self.first = first
8            self.middle = middle
9            self.last = last
10           self.house = house
11           self.name = f"{first} {middle} {last}"
12
13   def main():
14       student = get_student()
15       print(f"{student.name} from {student.house}")
16
17   def get_student():
18       first = input("First Name: ")
19       middle = input("Middle Name: ")
20       last = input("Last Name: ")
21       house = input("House: ")
22       return Student(first, middle, last, house)
23
24   if __name__ == "__main__":
25       main()
```

What if I only print "student" in the main function ?

```python
def main():
    student = get_student()
    print(student)
```

If we run the entire code with this modification, there will something like this:

py student.py

First Name: Renard

Middle Name: Gen

Last Name: Rose

House: Queens

<__main__.Student object at 0x000001A1E70DE710>

We don't need to explain this

We are going to introduce another method: __str__

In Python, __str__ is a special method, also known as a dunder method (short for "double underscore"), that defines how an object should be represented as a string when using the str() function or when the object is passed to print().

When you define the __str__ method within a class, you are essentially specifying how instances of that class should be converted to strings. This is particularly useful for providing a meaningful and human-readable representation of objects.

Example of how __str__ works:

```
1  class MyClass:
2      def __init__(self, x, y):
3          self.x = x
4          self.y = y
5
6      def __str__(self):
7          return f"MyClass instance with x={self.x} and y={self.y}"
8
9   obj = MyClass(3, 5)
10  print(obj)  # Output: MyClass instance with x=3 and y=5
```

In this example, the __str__ method is defined within the MyClass
class to return a string representation of the instance's attributes x
and y. When the print() function is called with an instance of
MyClass, Python automatically invokes the __str__ method to
obtain a string representation of the object.

By implementing the __str__ method, you can customize how
instances of your class are displayed as strings, making your code
more readable and informative.

```
1   class Student:
2       def __init__(self, name, house):
3           if not name:
4               raise ValueError("Missing Name")
5           if house not in ["Queens", "Bercy", "Sunset Beach", "Brighton"]:
6               raise ValueError("Invalid house")
7           self.name = name
8           self.house = house
9
10      def __str__(self):
11          return "a student"
12
13
14  def main():
15      student = get_student()
16      print(student)
17
18  def get_student():
19      name = input(" Name: ")
20      house = input("House: ")
21      return Student(name, house)
22
23  if __name__ == "__main__":
24      main()
```

py student.py
Name: Eric
House: Queens
a student
```
```

To avoid the generic output "a student", we must modify the print arguments.

```
1    class Student:
2        def __init__(self, name, house):
3            if not name:
4                raise ValueError("Missing Name")
5            if house not in ["Queens", "Bercy", "Sunset Beach", "Brighton"]
6                raise ValueError("Invalid house")
7            self.name = name
8            self.house = house
9
10       def __str__(self):
11           return f" {self.name} from {self.house}"
12
13
14   def main():
15       student = get_student()
16       print(student)
17
18   def get_student():
19       name = input(" Name: ")
20       house = input("House: ")
21       return Student(name, house)
22
23   if __name__ == "__main__":
24       main()
```

py student.py
Name: John
House: Bercy
John from Bercy

Maybe we would like to create more functionalities for our student.

Let's create a function, casting a charm

```
1    class Student:
2        def __init__(self, name, house, patronus):
3            if not name:
4                raise ValueError("Missing Name")
5            if house not in ['Queens', 'Bercy', "Sunset Beach", 'Brighton']:
6                raise ValueError("Invalid house")
7            self.name = name
8            self.house = house
9            self.patronus = patronus
10
11       def __str__(self):
12           return f"{self.name} from {self.house}"
13
14       def charm(self):
15           match self.patronus:
16               case "The Hyena":
17                   return """
18                       \        /
19                        \_____/
20                       /    \   """
21               case "German Shepherd":
22                   return """
23                       __
24                      / \__
25                   (\ /       \
26                    \ \__   __/ /
27                     \___\__/___/  """
28               case "Wolverine":
29                   return """
30                       ____
31                      /     \
32                     / *  * \
33                     \  O  O /
34                      \_____/
35                       / /
36                   __/ /_____  """
37               case _:
38                   return "/"
39
40
41   def main():
42       student = get_student()
43       print("Expecto Patronum!")
44       print(student.charm())
45
46   def get_student():
47       name = input(" Name: ")
48       house = input("House: ")
49       patronus = input("Patronus: ")
50       return Student(name, house, patronus)
51
52   if __name__ == "__main__":
53       main()
```

@property

In Python, **@property** is a built-in decorator that allows you to define methods that can be accessed like attributes. It allows you to create special getter methods that provide control over how attributes are accessed and modified.

How @property works:

Getter Method: You can use @property to define a method that behaves like a read-only attribute. This method will be called whenever the attribute is accessed.

Setter Method: Additionally, you can define a setter method using @<property_name>.setter decorator, which allows you to control how the attribute is modified.

Deleter Method: You can also define a deleter method using @<property_name>.deleter decorator, which allows you to define behavior when the attribute is deleted.

Example:

```
1    class Circle:
2        def __init__(self, radius):
3            self._radius = radius
4
5        @property
6        def radius(self):
7            return self._radius
8
9        @radius.setter
10       def radius(self, value):
11           if value < 0:
12               raise ValueError("Radius cannot be negative")
13           self._radius = value
14
15       @radius.deleter
16       def radius(self):
17           del self._radius
18
19   # Create a Circle object
20   c = Circle(5)
21
22   # Access the radius attribute like an attribute, but it's actually calling the getter method
23   print(c.radius)  # Output: 5
24
25   # Set the radius attribute using the setter method
26   c.radius = 10
27
28   # Delete the radius attribute using the deleter method
29   del c.radius
```

In this example:

The **@property** decorator defines a getter method radius that returns the value of the _radius attribute.

The **@radius.setter** decorator defines a setter method radius that allows setting the value of the _radius attribute. It performs validation to ensure that the radius cannot be negative.

The @radius.deleter decorator defines a deleter method radius that allows deleting the _radius attribute.

Using @property, you can encapsulate the logic for getting, setting, and deleting attributes within methods, providing more control and flexibility over how attributes are accessed and modified.

Decorators = functions that modify the behavior of other functions.

How to use this new function?

```python
    #Getter. A function from a class that gets
some attributes
    @property
    def house(self):
        return self.house

    @house.setter
    #Setter. A function from a class that sets some
values
    def house(self, house):
        self.house = house
```

```
1    class Student:
2        def __init__(self, name, house):
3            if not name:
4                raise ValueError("Missing Name")
5            self.name = name
6            self.house = house
7
8        def __str__(self):
9            return f" {self.name} from {self.house}"
10
11        #Getter. A function from a class that gets some attributes
12        @property
13        def house(self):
14            return self._house
15
16        #Setter. A function from a class that sets some values
17        @house.setter
18        def house(self, house):
19            if house not in ["Queens", "Bercy", "Sunset Beach", "Brighton"]:
20                raise ValueError("Invalid house")
21            self._house = house
22
23
24
25    def main():
26        student = get_student()
27        print(student)
28
29    def get_student():
30        name = input(" Name: ")
31        house = input("House: ")
32        return Student(name, house)
33
34    if __name__ == "__main__":
35        main()
```

In this code, **@property** and @**house.setter** decorators are used to create getter and setter methods for the house attribute of the Student class.

The reason for using self._house in the getter method instead of **self.house** is to avoid naming conflicts between the attribute and the getter method.

Here's the relevant part of the code:

```python
1    @property
2    def house(self):
3        return self._house
4
5    @house.setter
6    def house(self, house):
7        if house not in ["Queens", "Bercy", "Sunset Beach", "Brighton"]:
8            raise ValueError("Invalid house")
```

In this code:

The getter method house returns the value of the **_house** attribute.

The setter method house sets the value of the **_house** attribute after performing validation

By convention, when using properties in Python, it's a common practice to prefix the name of the actual attribute with an underscore (_) to indicate that it's intended to be private or internal to the class. This helps prevent accidental access or modification of the attribute directly from outside the class.

Nevertheless, when we come back to our code and test it:

py student.py

 Name: Eric
House: Queens
Eric from Queens

```python
1   class Student:
2       def __init__(self, name, house):
3           self.name = name
4           self.house = house
5
6       def __str__(self):
7           return f" {self.name} from {self.house}"
8
9       @property
10      def name(self):
11          return self._name
12
13      @name.setter
14      def name(self, name):
15          if not name:
16              raise ValueError("Missing name")
17          self._name = name
18
19
20       #Getter.
21      @property
22      def house(self):
23          return self._house
24
25      #Setter
26      @house.setter
27      def house(self, house):
28          if house not in ["Queens", "Bercy", "Sunset Beach", "Brighton"]:
29              raise ValueError("Invalid house")
30          self._house = house
31
32
33
34  def main():
35      student = get_student()
36      print(student)
37
38  def get_student():
39      name = input(" Name: ")
40      house = input("House: ")
41      return Student(name, house)
42
43  if __name__ == "__main__":
44      main()
```

133

Class Methods

Class Methods:

@classmethod

A class method in Python is a method that is bound to the class itself rather than an instance of the class. This means that class methods can be called on the class itself, rather than on instances of the class. Class methods are defined using the **@classmethod** decorator.

Characteristics of class methods:

Bound to Class: Class methods are bound to the class itself and can access class variables and other class-level attributes.

First Argument: The first argument of a class method is conventionally named **cls**, which refers to the class itself. This allows the class method to access and modify class-level attributes.

Can Be Accessed via Instances: While class methods are typically called on the class itself, they can also be called on instances of the class. When called on an instance, the instance is automatically passed as the first argument (**cls**).

Common Use Cases: Class methods are commonly used for alternative constructors, factory methods, or methods that operate on class-level data rather than instance-level data.

@classmethod is another decorator, another function that you can use to specify that this method is not by default implicitly instance that has access to the object itself.

Here's an example to illustrate the definition and usage of a class method:

```
1    class MyClass:
2        class_variable = 10
3
4        def __init__(self, value):
5            self.value = value
6
7        @classmethod
8        def from_string(cls, string):
9            # This is a class method that acts as an alternative constructor
10           # It creates a new instance of MyClass from a string
11           return cls(int(string))  # Create an instance with the integer value of the string
12
13       @classmethod
14       def increment_class_variable(cls, increment):
15           # This is a class method that increments the class variable
16           cls.class_variable += increment
17
18   # Creating an instance using the class method from_string
19   obj1 = MyClass.from_string("5")
20   print(obj1.value)  # Output: 5
21
22   # Accessing the class variable directly
23   print(MyClass.class_variable)  # Output: 10
24
25   # Calling the class method to increment the class variable
26   MyClass.increment_class_variable(5)
27   print(MyClass.class_variable)  # Output: 15
```

code hat.py

This hat is to decide what house a student is in.

First Step:
```
class Hat:
    ... # I know that i want a Hat class, but don't
know yet what i want to do in

# What functionalities?
# Create a variable and instantiate an object

hat = Hat()
hat.sort("Eric")
```

135

Second Step:
Let's initialize that class

```
1   class Hat:
2       def sort(self, name):
3           print(name, "is in", "some house")
4
5   hat = Hat()
6   hat.sort("Eric")
```

py hat.py

Eric is in some house

Now we want to introduce a little random list and choosing the house for Eric randomly

```
1   import random
2
3   class Hat:
4       def __init__(self):
5           self.houses = ["Queens", "Bercy", "Sunset Beach", "Brighton"]
6
7   #We replace "some house" with the actual house
8
9       def sort(self, name):
10          house = random.choice(self.houses)
11          print(name, "is in", house)
12
13  hat = Hat()
14  hat.sort("Eric")
```

py hat.py

Eric is in Queens

We could simplify the **sort( )** function:

```
def sort(self, name):
    print(name, "is in",
random.choice(self.houses))
```
Class variables: exist within class itself, and there is just one copy of that variable for all of the objects

136

```
1    import random
2
3    class Hat:
4        houses = ["Queens", "Bercy", "Sunset Beach", "Brighton"]
5
6        # I can change "self" to be just class
7        # Because houses is now not instance variables accessible by self.house
8        # It is now a class variable accessible by cls.houses
9
10       @classmethod
11       def sort(cls, name):
12           print(name, "is in", random.choice(cls.houses))
13
14   # Here, i am not instantiating
15   # But just access a class method inside of a Hat class
16
17   Hat.sort("Eric")
```

py hat.py

Eric is in Brighton

We can try this code, and it still works.

When our code is getting longer, it's just a way of encapsulating our data, functionalities, inside things that have names called classes.

```
1    import random
2
3    houses = ["Queens", "Bercy", "Sunset Beach", "Brighton"]
4
5    def sort(name):
6        print(name, "is in", random.choice(houses))
7    sort("Eric")
```

py hat.py

Eric is in Sunset Beach

Let's re-open our python file: student.py and see how it is really structured.

```python
1   class Student:
2       def __init__(self, name, house):
3           self.name = name
4           self.house = house
5
6       def __str__(self):
7           return f" {self.name} from {self.house}"
8
9       @property
10      def name(self):
11          return self._name
12
13      @name.setter
14      def name(self, name):
15          if not name:
16              raise ValueError("Missing name")
17          self._name = name
18
19      #Getter.
20      @property
21      def house(self):
22          return self._house
23
24      #Setter
25      @house.setter
26      def house(self, house):
27          if house not in ["Queens", "Bercy", "Sunset Beach", "Brighton"]:
28              raise ValueError("Invalid house")
29          self._house = house
30
31  def main():
32      student = get_student()
33      print(student)
34
35  def get_student():
36      name = input(" Name: ")
37      house = input("House: ")
38      return Student(name, house)
39
40  if __name__ == "__main__":
41      main()
```

We clean property and setter

get_student( ) function can be deleted

138

```
1   class Student:
2       def __init__(self, name, house):
3           self.name = name
4           self.house = house
5
6       def __str__(self):
7           return f" {self.name} from {self.house}"
8
9       # I can call this method without instantiating student object first
10      @classmethod
11      def get(cls):
12          name = input("Name: ")
13          house = input("House: ")
14          return cls(name, house)
15
16  def main():
17      student = Student.get()
18      print(student)
19
20  if __name__ == "__main__":
21      main()
```

py hat.py

Eric from Brighton

@static method

A static method in Python is a method that is bound to the class itself rather than an instance of the class. Unlike instance methods and class methods, static methods do not have access to the class or instance attributes. Static methods are defined using the @staticmethod decorator.

Static methods:

Characteristics of static methods:

Bound to Class: Like class methods, static methods are bound to the class itself rather than an instance of the class.

No Access to Class or Instance Attributes: Static methods do not have access to the class or instance attributes. They behave like regular functions and do not receive any implicit arguments.

Common Use Cases: Static methods are commonly used when a method does not depend on class or instance state. They are useful for grouping functions related to the class within the class namespace.

Example:

```
1    class MathOperations:
2        @staticmethod
3        def add(x, y):
4            # This is a static method that adds two numbers
5            return x + y
6
7        @staticmethod
8        def multiply(x, y):
9            # This is a static method that multiplies two numbers
10           return x * y
11
12   # Calling static methods directly on the class
13   sum_result = MathOperations.add(5, 3)
14   product_result = MathOperations.multiply(5, 3)
15
16   print("Sum:", sum_result)         # Output: Sum: 8
17   print("Product:", product_result) # Output: Product: 15
```

In this example:

add and multiply are static methods defined within the MathOperations class using the @staticmethod decorator.

Static methods add and multiply do not require access to class or instance attributes, so they are defined as static methods.

Static methods can be called directly on the class (MathOperations.add(...), MathOperations.multiply(...)), without the need to create an instance of the class.

Inheritance

Let's open a new python file:

code wizard.py

Let's define a class named **"Student"**

```
1    class Student:
2        def __init__(self, name, house):
3            self.name = name
4            self.house = house
5
6    class Professor:
7        def __init__(self, name, subject):
8            self.name = name
9            self.subject = subject
```

We might need to add a ValueError for the two classes:

```
class Student:
    def __init__(self, name, house):
        if not name:
            raise ValueError("Missing name")
.............................

class Professor:
    def __init__(self, name, subject):
        if not name:
            raise ValueError("Missing name")
```

But we know that OOP supports multiclass. We define a third class that have common attributes.

```
1   class Wizard:
2       def __init__(self, name):
3           if not name:
4               raise ValueError("Missing name")
5           self.name = name
6
7   class Student(Wizard):
8           def __init__(self, name, house):
9               super().__init__(name)
10              self.house = house
11
12  class Professor(Wizard):
13      def __init__(self, name, subject):
14          super().__init__(name)
15          self.subject = subject
16
17  wizard = Wizard("Gandi")
18  student = Student("Eric", "Bercy")
19  prefessor = Professor("Ron", "Travelling to Chicago in Summer")
```

OPERATOR OVERLOADING

Let's open a new python file: code vault.py

```
1 ∨ class Vault:
2 ∨     def __init__(self, galleons=0, sickles=0, knuts=0):
3           self.galleons = galleons
4           self.sickles = sickles
5           self.knuts = knuts
6
7   potter = Vault(75,14,91)
```

py vault.py

<__main__.Vault object at 0x000001EE2A9CDE90>

Let's modify our code:

```
1   class Vault:
2       def __init__(self, galleons=0, sickles=0, knuts=0):
3           self.galleons = galleons
4           self.sickles = sickles
5           self.knuts = knuts
6
7       def __str__(self):
8           return f"{self.galleons} Galleons,{self.sickles} Sickles, {self.knuts} knuts"
9
10  potter = Vault(75,14,91)
11  print(potter)
```

py vault.py

75 Galleons,14 Sickles, 91 knuts

Define another variable:

```python
1   class Vault:
2       def __init__(self, galleons=0, sickles=0, knuts=0):
3           self.galleons = galleons
4           self.sickles = sickles
5           self.knuts = knuts
6
7       def __str__(self):
8           return f"{self.galleons} Galleons,{self.sickles} Sickles, {self.knuts} knuts"
9
10  potter = Vault(75,14,91)
11  print(potter)
12
13  weasley = Vault(55,17,98)
14  print(weasley)
```

py vault.py

75 Galleons,14 Sickles, 91 knuts
55 Galleons,17 Sickles, 98 knuts

Let's do some additions:

```python
1   class Vault:
2       def __init__(self, galleons=0, sickles=0, knuts=0):
3           self.galleons = galleons
4           self.sickles = sickles
5           self.knuts = knuts
6
7       def __str__(self):
8           return f"{self.galleons} Galleons,{self.sickles} Sickles, {self.knuts} knuts"
9
10  potter = Vault(75,14,91)
11  print(potter)
12
13  weasley = Vault(55,17,98)
14  print(weasley)
15
16  galleons = potter.galleons + weasley.galleons
17  sickles = potter.sickles + weasley.sickles
18  knuts = potter.knuts + weasley.knuts
19  total = Vault(galleons,sickles,knuts)
20  print(total)
```

py vault.py

75 Galleons,14 Sickles, 91 knuts
55 Galleons,17 Sickles, 98 knuts
130 Galleons,31 Sickles, 189 knuts

docs.python.org/3/reference/datamodel.html#special-method-name

object._add_(self, other)

We are going to "teach" python how to add two vaults together

```python
class Vault:
    def __init__(self, galleons=0, sickles=0, knuts=0):
        self.galleons = galleons
        self.sickles = sickles
        self.knuts = knuts

    def __str__(self):
        return f"{self.galleons} Galleons,{self.sickles} Sickles, {self.knuts} knuts"


    def __add__(self, other):
        galleons = self.galleons + other.galleons
        sickles = self.sickles + other.sickles
        knuts = self.knuts + other.knuts
        return Vault(galleons, sickles, knuts)

potter = Vault(75,14,91)
print(potter)

weasley = Vault(55,17,98)
print(weasley)

total = potter + weasley
print(total)
```

py vault.py

75 Galleons,14 Sickles, 91 knuts
55 Galleons,17 Sickles, 98 knuts
130 Galleons,31 Sickles, 189 knuts

Set: collection of values where there is no duplicate

docs.python.org/3/howto/

docs.python.org/3/library/stdtypes.html

Let's create a new python file: code **houses.py**

```
1   students = [
2   {"name": "Yanis", "house": "Bercy"},
3   {"name": "Eric", "house": "Bercy"},
4   {"name": "Terry", "house": "Bercy"},
5   {"name": "Peter", "house": "Queens"}
6   ]
7
8   houses =[] # Every time i iterate, i will add a house if i haven't seen it before
9
10  for student in students:
11      if student["house"] not in houses:
12          houses.append(student["house"])
13
14  for house in sorted(houses):
15      print(house)
```

python houses.py

Dcroy

Queens

We can see here that we don't have duplicates

Let's create an empty set

```
1   students = [
2   {"name": "Yanis", "house": "Bercy"},
3   {"name": "Eric", "house": "Bercy"},
4   {"name": "Terry", "house": "Bercy"},
5   {"name": "Peter", "house": "Queens"}
6   ]
7
8   houses = set()
9
10  for student in students:
11      houses.add(student["house"]) # add() doesn't allow duplicates
12
13  for house in sorted(houses):
14      print(house)
```

python houses.py
Bercy
Queens

Let's create a new python file: code bank.py

```
1    balance = 0
2
3  ∨ def main():
4  |      print("Balance:", balance)
5
6  ∨ if __name__ == "__main__":
7  |      main()
```

We can test by running bank.py

```
1    balance = 0
2
3    def main():
4        print("Balance:", balance)
5        deposit(100)
6        withdraw(50)
7        print("Balance:", balance)
8
9    def deposit(n):
10       balance += n
11
12   def withdraw(n):
13   |    balance -= n
14
15   if __name__ == "__main__":
16       main()
```

python bank.py

Balance: 0
Traceback (most recent call last):
  File "bank.py", line 16, in <module>
    main()
  File "bank.py", line 5, in main
    deposit(100)
  File "bank.py", line 10, in deposit
    balance += n
**UnboundLocalError: local variable 'balance' referenced before
assignment**

147

Here, we need to make some modifications:

Let's take the global variable inside of "main" function. If we do this, it won't work.

What we have to do here is to add the key word "global"

```
1    balance = 0
2
3    def main():
4        print("Balance:", balance)
5        deposit(100)
6        withdraw(50)
7        print("Balance:", balance)
8
9    def deposit(n):
10       global balance
11       balance += n
12
13   def withdraw(n):
14       global balance
15       balance -= n
16
17   if __name__ == "__main__":
18       main()
```

python bank.py

Balance: 0

Balance: 50

We want to encapsulate our code in a class

```python
 1  class Account:
 2      def __init__(self):
 3          self._balance = 0 # The underscore is to visualy indicate that it's private
 4
 5      @property
 6      def balance(self):
 7          return self._balance
 8
 9      def deposit(self, n):
10          self._balance +=n
11
12      def withdraw(self, n):
13          self._balance -=n
14
15  def main():
16      account = Account()
17      print("Balance:", account.balance)
18      account.deposit(100)
19      account.withdraw(50)
20      print("Balance:", account.balance)
21
22  if __name__ == "__main__":
23      main()
```

python bank.py

Balance: 0

Balance: 50

We open a new python file: code laugh.py

```
1    #Sam laughes 3 times
2    for _ in range(3):
3    |    print("haha")
```

py laugh.py

haha

haha

haha

```
1    LAUGH    ]
2    for _ in range(LAUGH):
3    |    print("haha")
```

py laugh.py

haha

haha

haha

```
1    class Sam:
2        LAUGH = 3
3
4        def laugh(self):
5            for _ in range(Sam.LAUGH):
6                print("haha")
7
8    sam = Sam()
9    sam.laugh()
```

py laugh.py

haha

haha

haha

TYPE HINTS

Type hints:

docs.python.org/3/library/typing.html

Type hints in Python are annotations added to function parameters and return values to indicate the expected types. They provide additional information about the types of variables used in a function, making the code more readable and self-documenting. While type hints are optional and do not affect the runtime behavior of the code, they can be helpful for improving code clarity, enabling static type checkers, and providing better IDE support for code completion and error detection.

Type hints are specified using the following syntax:

For parameters: parameter_name: type

For return values: -> return_type

Example of using type hints in Python:

```
1    def add(x: int, y: int) -> int:
2        return x + y
3
4    result: int = add(5, 3)
5    print(result)  # Output: 8
```

MYPY

mypy -> what is it?

Mypy is an optional static type checker for Python. It analyzes Python programs and detects type-related errors or inconsistencies at compile time, helping developers find bugs and write more robust code. Mypy allows you to add type hints to your Python code and performs static type checking based on these annotations.

Let's first install by running from the Terminal: **pip install mypy**

Maybe by installing "mypy" with "pip install mypy" you may encounter some issues

If, so... it might be the "exe" (mypy.exe and mypyc.exe) file located in the directory:
C:\Users\my_name\AppData\Roaming\Python\Python311\Scripts

You copy these files and you paste them in

C:\Programfiles\Python311\Scripts

Your directories might be different from mines

Web site: mypy.readthedocs.io

```
1    def laugh(n):
2        for _ in range(n):
3            print("haha")
4
5    number = input("Number: ")
6    laugh(number)
```

py laugh.py

Number: 4

Traceback (most recent call last):

  File "C:\Users\jerom\laugh.py", line 6, in <module>

   laugh(number)

  File "C:\Users\jerom\laugh.py", line 2, in laugh

  for _ in range(n):

    ^^^^^^^^

TypeError: 'str' object cannot be interpreted as an integer

There is a typeError here. So what can we do about it?

```
1    def laugh(n: int):
2        for _ in range(n):
3            print("haha")
4
5    number = input("Number: ")
6    laugh(number)
```

mypy laugh.py

laugh.py:5: error: Incompatible types in assignment (expression has type "str", variable has type "int") [assignment]

Found 1 error in 1 file (checked 1 source file)

Thanks to "mypy", we can already see what's wrong, what kind of error that we've got here.

I'm expecting a "int" but it returned me a "str"

```
1    def laugh(n: int):
2        for _ in range(n):
3            print("haha")
4
5    number: int = int(input("Number: "))
6    laugh(number)
```

```
$ mypy laugh.py
Success: no issues found in 1 source file
```

Now after correcting our error, we have this output

```
$ py laugh.py
Number: 4
haha
haha
haha
haha
```

If I added these lines without really paying attention:

```
1    def laugh(n: int) -> None:
2        for _ in range(n):
3            print("haha")
4
5    number: int = int(input("Number: "))
6    laughs: str = laugh(number)
7    print(laughs)
```

py laugh.py

Number: 3
haha
haha
haha
None

I don't really want to have this "None".

```
$ mypy laugh.py
laugh.py:6: error: "laugh" does not return a value (it only ever returns None)  [func-returns-value]
Found 1 error in 1 file (checked 1 source file)
```

Now a corrected version

```
1    def laugh(n: int) -> str:
2        return "haha\n"*n
3
4    number: int = int(input("Number: "))
5    laughs: str = laugh(number)
6    print(laughs, end = "")
```

py laugh.py

Number: 3
haha
haha
haha
haha

DOCSTRINGS

Docstrings

peps.python.org/pep-0257/

Standardize how you should document your function among other functions of your code.

A docstring, short for "documentation string," is a string literal that occurs as the first statement in a module, function, class, or method definition in Python. Its purpose is to provide documentation about the object it precedes.

Docstrings are typically enclosed in triple quotes (''' or """) and can span multiple lines. They serve as a form of inline documentation, helping developers understand the purpose, usage, and behavior of the associated code.

Here's an example of a docstring for a function:

```
1    def greet(name):
2        '''This function greets the user with the provided name.'''
3        print(f"Hello, {name}!")
```

In this example, the docstring '''This function greets the user with the provided name.''' provides information about what the greet function does.

Docstrings are particularly useful for generating documentation automatically, as they can be accessed programmatically using Python's built-in help() function or various documentation generation tools.

Let's modify our python file

code laugh.py

This Python script checks the length of the sys.argv list, which contains command-line arguments passed to the script. If the length of sys.argv is 1, it means that only the script name itself was provided as an argument (i.e., no additional arguments were passed).

If there are no additional arguments, the script prints "haha".

If there are additional arguments, it prints "Usage: laugh.py", indicating how the script should be used.

```
1    import sys
2
3    if len(sys.argv) == 1:
4        print("haha")
5    else:
6        print("Usage: laugh.py")
```

py laugh.py 3
Usage: laugh.py
py laugh.py
haha

```
1    import sys
2
3    if len(sys.argv) == 1:
4        print("haha")
5    elif len(sys.arg) == 3 and sys.argv[1] == "-n":
6        n = int(sys.argv[2])
7        for _ in range(n):
8            print("haha")
9    else:
10       print("Usage: laugh.py")
```

py laugh.py -n 3
haha
haha
haha
py laugh.py -n 2
haha
haha

ARGPARSE

Argparse:

argparse is a Python module in the standard library that provides a mechanism for parsing command-line arguments. It simplifies the process of building command-line interfaces (CLIs) by handling argument parsing, validation, help generation, and more.

With argparse, you can define the expected command-line arguments and options for your script or application, and argparse will parse the arguments provided by the user according to your specifications.

Key features of argparse:

Declarative Interface: You define the expected command-line arguments, options, and their types in a declarative way, using Python code.

Automatic Help Generation: argparse automatically generates help messages based on our argument definitions, making it easy for users to understand how to use your script.

Type Conversion and Validation: argparse handles type conversion and validation of command-line arguments, ensuring that the provided arguments meet the expected criteria.

Sub-commands: argparse supports sub-commands, allowing you to create complex command-line interfaces with hierarchical structures.

To parse arguments means to read it.

Example of using argparse to parse command-line arguments:

```
1   import argparse
2
3   parser = argparse.ArgumentParser(description='A simple script with argparse')
4
5   # Add positional argument
6   parser.add_argument('name', type=str, help='Name of the user')
7
8   # Add optional argument
9   parser.add_argument('--age', type=int, default=0, help='Age of the user')
10
11  # Parse the command-line arguments
12  args = parser.parse_args()
13
14  # Access the parsed arguments
15  print(f"Hello, {args.name}! You are {args.age} years old.")
```

In this example, the script defines a positional argument name and an optional argument --age. When the script is run with appropriate arguments, argparse will parse them and make them available through the args object.

```
1   import argparse
2
3   parser = argparse.ArgumentParser()
4   parser.add_argument("-n")
5   args = parser.parse_args()
6
7   for _ in range(int(args.n)):
8       print("haha")
```

```
$ py laugh.py -n 3
haha
haha
haha
```

```
1    import argparse
2
3    parser = argparse.ArgumentParser(description="Laugh like a fool" )
4    parser.add_argument("-n", default=1, help="number of times to laugh", type=int)
5    args = parser.parse_args()
6
7    for _ in range(int(args.n)):
8    |    print("haha")
```

py laugh.py --help

usage: laugh.py [-h] [-n N]

Laugh like a fool

options:

 -h, --help show this help message and exit

 -n N   number of times to laugh

py laugh.py -n 3

haha

haha

haha

UNPACKING

Unpacking :

Let's open a new file: code unpack.py

```
1    first, last = input("What's your name?").split(" ")
2    print(f"hello, {first}")
3
4    first, _ = input("What's your name?").split(" ")
5    print(f"hello, {first}")
```

python unpack.py
What's your name?Robert young
hello, Robert
What's your name?Annie Lovely
hello, Annie

```
1    def total(galleons, sickles, knuts):
2        return(galleons * 13 + sickles) * 33 + knuts
3
4    print(total(100,50,25)), "knuts"
```

python unpack.py

44575

```
1    def total(galleons, sickles, knuts):
2        return(galleons * 13 + sickles) * 33 + knuts
3
4    print(total(87,12,68), "knuts")
```

python unpack.py

37787 knuts

161

```
1    def total(galleons, sickles, knuts):
2        return(galleons * 13 + sickles) * 33 + knuts
3
4    coins = [87,12,68]
5
6    print(total(coins [0], coins[1], coins[2]), "knuts")
```

python unpack.py

37787 knuts

If I did this: print(total(coins), "knuts"), it would not have worked.

I should do this: print(total(*coins), "knuts")

```
1    def total(galleons, sickles, knuts):
2        return(galleons * 13 + sickles) * 33 + knuts
3
4    coins = [87,12,68]
5
6    print(total(*coins), "knuts")
```

python unpack.py

37787 knuts

```
1    def total(galleons, sickles, knuts):
2        return(galleons * 13 + sickles) * 33 + knuts
3
4    print(total(galleons=87, sickles=12, knuts=68), "knuts")
```

python unpack.py

37787 knuts

```
1    def total(galleons, sickles, knuts):
2        return(galleons * 13 + sickles) * 33 + knuts
3
4    coins = {"galleons":87, "sickles":12, "knuts":68}
5
6    print(total(coins["galleons"], coins["sickles"], coins["knuts"]), "knuts
```

python unpack.py

37787 knuts

```
1    def total(galleons, sickles, knuts):
2        return(galleons * 13 + sickles) * 33 + knuts
3
4    coins = {"galleons":87, "sickles":12, "knuts":68}
5
6    print(total(coins["galleons"], coins["sickles"], coins["knuts"]), "knut
```

python unpack.py

37787 knuts

*args, **kwargs

*args and **kwargs are special syntax in Python used to pass a variable number of arguments to a function or method.

*args: This syntax allows a function to accept any number of positional arguments. The *args parameter collects any number of positional arguments passed to the function into a tuple. It's often used when you want to create a function that can accept a variable number of arguments without explicitly specifying them.

**kwargs: This syntax allows a function to accept any number of keyword arguments. The **kwargs parameter collects any keyword arguments passed to the function into a dictionary. It's often used when you want to create a function that can accept a variable number of named arguments without explicitly specifying them.

Here's a simple example demonstrating the usage of ***args** and ****kwargs**:

```
1   def example_function(*args, **kwargs):
2       print("Positional arguments (*args):", args)
3       print("Keyword arguments (**kwargs):", kwargs)
4
5   # Calling the function with different arguments
6   example_function(1, 2, 3, name='Alice', age=30)
7
```

The output:

```
Positional arguments (*args): (1, 2, 3)
Keyword arguments (**kwargs): {'name':
'Alice', 'age': 30}
```

In this example, ***args** collects the positional arguments (1, 2, 3) into a tuple, and ****kwargs** collects the keyword arguments {'name': 'Alice', 'age': 30} into a dictionary. This allows the function example_function to accept any number of positional and keyword arguments

```
1    def f(*args, **kwargs):
2        print("Positional: ", args)
3
4    f(87, 12, 68)
```

python unpack.py

Positional: (87, 12, 68)

```
1    def f(*args, **kwargs):
2        print("Named: ", kwargs)
3
4    f(galleons=87, sickles=12, knuts=68)
```

python unpack.py

Named: {'galleons': 87, 'sickles': 12, 'knuts': 68}

Let's open a new file:

code yell.py

```
1    def main():
2        yell(["i", "like", "swimming"])
3
4    def yell(words):
5        uppercased = []
6        for word in words:
7            uppercased.append(word.upper())
8        print(*uppercased)
9
10   if __name__ =="__main__":
11       main()
```

py yell.py

I LIKE SWIMMING

Try to replace print(*uppercased) by print(uppercased)

166

FUNCTION: map()

Map function: map(function, iterable)

The map() function in Python is a built-in function that applies a specified function to each item in an iterable (such as a list, tuple, or dictionary) and returns an iterator that yields the results.

The general syntax of the map() function is:

map(function, iterable)

function: A function that will be applied to each item in the iterable.

iterable: An iterable (e.g., list, tuple) whose elements will be processed by the function.

The map() function applies the specified function to each element of the iterable and returns an iterator containing the results. It's a way to perform element-wise operations on an iterable without using explicit loops.

Here's a simple example of using the map() function:

```
1   # Define a function
2   def square(x):
3       return x * x
4
5   # Apply the function to each element in the list using map()
6   numbers = [1, 2, 3, 4, 5]
7   squared_numbers = map(square, numbers)
8
9   # Convert the iterator to a list to see the results
10  print(list(squared_numbers))  # Output: [1, 4, 9, 16, 25]
```

In this example, the **square()** function is applied to each element in the numbers list using the map() function. The result is an iterator containing the squared values of the original elements. We convert the iterator to a list to see the results more clearly.

```
1    def main():
2    |    yell("i", "like", "swimming")
3
4    def yell(*words):
5        uppercased = map(str.upper, words)
6        print(*uppercased)
7
8    if __name__ == "__main__":
9        main()
```

py yell.py

I LIKE SWIMMING

List comprehensions

```
1    def main():
2        yell("i", "like", "swimming")
3
4    def yell(*words):
5        uppercased = [word.upper() for word in words]
6        print(*uppercased)
7
8    if __name__ == "__main__":
9    |    main()
```

py yell.py

I LIKE SWIMMING

Let's open a new python file: code queens.py

```
1    students = [
2    {"name": "Yanis", "house": "Bercy"},
3    {"name": "Eric", "house": "Bercy"},
4    {"name": "Terry", "house": "Bercy"},
5    {"name": "Peter", "house": "Queens"}
6    ]
7
8    bercys = [
9        student["name"] for student in students if student["house"] == "Bercy"
10   ]
11   for bercy in sorted(bercys):
12       print(bercy)
```

python bercys.py

Eric

Terry

Yanis

Function(filter, iterable)

```
1    students = [
2    {"name": "Yanis", "house": "Bercy"},
3    {"name": "Eric", "house": "Bercy"},
4    {"name": "Terry", "house": "Bercy"},
5    {"name": "Peter", "house": "Queens"}
6    ]
7
8    def is_bercy(s):
9        return s["house"] == "Bercy"
10
11   bercys = filter(is_bercy, students)
12
13   for bercy in sorted(bercys, key=lambda s: s["name"]):
14       print(bercy["name"])
```

python bercys.py

Eric

Terry

Dictionary comprehensions

We create a list of a dictionary

```
1    students = ["Yanis", "Eric", "Terry"]
2
3    bercys = []
4
5    for student in students:
6    |    bercys.append({"name":student, "house":"Bercy"})
7    print(bercys)
```

python bercys.py

[{'name': 'Yanis', 'house': 'Bercy'}, {'name': 'Eric', 'house': 'Bercy'}, {'name': 'Terry', 'house': 'Bercy'}]

We can do the same in a succinct way

```
1    students = ["Yanis", "Eric", "Terry"]
2
3    bercys = [{"name":student, "house": "Bercy"} for student in students]
4    print(bercys)
```

python bercys.py

[{'name': 'Yanis', 'house': 'Bercy'}, {'name': 'Eric', 'house': 'Bercy'}, {'name': 'Terry', 'house': 'Bercy'}]

Another version

```
1    students = ["Yanis", "Eric", "Terry"]
2
3    bercys = {student:"Bercy" for student in students}
4    print(bercys)
```

python bercys.py

{'Yanis': 'Bercy', 'Eric': 'Bercy', 'Terry': 'Bercy'}

```
1    students = ["Yanis", "Eric",  "Terry"]
2
3    bercys = []
4
5    for i in range(len(students)):
6    |    print(i+1, students[i])
```

python bercys.py

1 Yanis

2 Eric

3 Terry

FUNCTION: enumerate()

enumerate(iterable, start=0)

```
1    students = ["Yanis", "Eric",  "Terry"]
2
3    for i, student in enumerate(students):
4    |    print(i+1, student)
```

python bercys.py

1 Yanis

2 Eric

3 Terry

GENERATORS

Generators

In Python, a generator is a special type of iterator that can be used to generate a sequence of values lazily, on-the-fly, without needing to store the entire sequence in memory. Generators are implemented using functions and the yield statement.

Characteristics of generators:

Lazy Evaluation: Generators produce values only when requested They generate values one at a time and only when needed, which can be more memory-efficient compared to creating a list or tuple containing all values upfront.

Memory Efficiency: Generators generate values on-the-fly, so they do not require storing the entire sequence in memory. This makes them suitable for processing large or infinite sequences.

Iteration Support: Generators can be iterated over using loops or other iterable-consuming constructs (e.g., list comprehensions, sum(), max()). They can also be passed directly to functions that expect iterable objects.

Stateful Iteration: Generators can maintain internal state between calls. The state of a generator function is preserved across successive calls to next() or iteration loops.

Generators are typically implemented using generator functions or generator expressions:

Generator Functions: These are functions that contain one or more yield statements. When called, a generator function returns a generator object, which can be used to iterate over the values produced by the function.

Generator Expressions: These are similar to list comprehensions but use parentheses instead of square brackets. They create anonymous generator objects that produce values as needed.

Example:

```
1    def squares(n):
2        for i in range(n):
3            yield i * i
4
5    # Create a generator object
6    gen = squares(5)
7
```

In this example, the **squares()** function is a generator function that yields the squares of numbers from 0 to n-1. When the generator object gen is iterated over, it generates the square values lazily, one at a time, until exhaustion.

Let's open a new python file: code doors.py

```
1    def main():
2        n = int(input("What's n?"))
3        for i in range(n):
4            print(" ▮ " * i)
5
6    if __name__ == "__main__":
7        main()
```

py doors.py

What's n?4

```
 1    def main():
 2        n = int(input("What's n?"))
 3        for i in range(n):
 4            print(door(i))
 5
 6    def door(n):
 7        return "🚪" * n
 8
 9    if __name__ == "__main__":
10        main()
```

py doors.py

What's n?5

```
 1    def main():
 2        n = int(input("What's n?"))
 3        for s in door(n):
 4            print(s)
 5
 6    def door(n):
 7        flock = []
 8        for i in range(n):
 9            flock.append("🚪" * n)
10        return flock
11
12    if __name__ == "__main__":
13        main()
```

py doors.py

What's n?6

174

If n = 100000, my program stops, just because it is a huge number of images, it returns all the images at once. Solution, use a generator, to generate one image at a time.

Key word: yield -> to generate one value at a time

```
1    def main():
2        n = int(input("What's n?"))
3        for s in door(n):
4            print(s)
5
6    def door(n):
7        for i in range(n):
8            yield(" █ " * n)
9
10   if __name__ == "__main__":
11       main()
```

python doors.py

Try to test for n = 1000000

A little summary of what we've seen

Functions, Variables

Conditionals

Loops

Exceptions

Libraries

Unit Tests

File I/O

Regular Expressions

Object Oriented Programing

Various

Python is a vast world with endless possibilities. So, my advice is simply to practice, practice, practice, and never stop practicing. Take the time to read the documentation. Try building your own functions, applications, etc. Remember that mastering Python requires time and perseverance, but the skills you develop along the way will open doors to exciting opportunities in the programming field. Don't be afraid to explore, experiment, and tackle challenges, as this is how you'll develop your expertise and creativity in the world of Python. Good luck on your learning journey!